Every Child An Achiever

A Parent's Guide to the Kumon Method

One of my children came home one day and announced that she was really dumb in math. I said 'No, honey, you're not dumb, and you're not bad in math; you just need a little practice. Mommy will work with you.' She said no, she didn't want Mommy to help her, she wanted to go to Kumon like her friends did. I didn't even know what it was, but I found out pretty quick, and it sounded good. I called the local instructor, enrolled her in the class, and she just took off. She loves it. I can't tell you... She's in the 6th grade at school and doing Level H [8th grade algebra] now. Her younger brother watched her do it for a few months, then he started begging me to let him do Kumon too. My husband and I found it a little hard to believe—you know, your kids begging you to let them study more—but we put him in the same center, and now he loves it. It's a parent's dream come true.

—Barbara Maxwell, mother, Texas

I feel more at ease taking tests [in school] than I've ever felt before. Right now I'm doing square roots; I usually finish a test quickly, before other kids do; then I go back and check it over, then I hand it in and start doing other work.

—Nicholas Terzani, 12, Connecticut

Our older son is in high school, and he'd become calculator-dependent. He was using it for everything. One night he was working on a math problem involving reducing fractions, and my daughter, who is much younger and studying in Kumon, was watching him. He just started plugging the numbers into his calculator. His little sister grabbed the calculator away from him and shouted "What are you doing? If you can't reduce fractions without a calculator you don't belong in algebra!" After that I put him in Kumon, too. They made him start at Level A, which he didn't like at first, but while he hates to admit it, he says it really did help him.

—Leslie Gould, mother, Ohio

What's good about Kumon is that you learn stuff, and you learn it really well, then you learn it again in school, which means you get good review.

—John Liu, 10, San Francisco

When Michael was in kindergarten we met some parents who had their kids in Kumon, and after talking to them we decided to start him in the program, too. About a year later we put his little sister in. Now other parents are discovering that our kids are tops in their math classes, and they're asking us what we're doing that's special. We tell them it's just Kumon. I think it's great. We recommend it to everybody.

—Betty Christiansen, mother, California

I love the feeling when you pass the test at the end of a level and you go on to the next level. Before, I used to like multiplication and division a lot, but now I like reducing fractions more than anything.

—Robin Cray, 3rd Grade, Los Angeles

I know there are some parents who send their kids to Kumon for remedial purposes, meaning the child has some problem with math. That wasn't our situation at all. We joined because we saw it as an enrichment program, something that would help to build a certain level of confidence and skill for our kids. And we were not disappointed. Both of our children are now in a school for gifted children, a school that requires special examinations to enter, and they're both excelling in math even at that school. I would have to say it's because of their experience in Kumon that they're ahead of everyone else. The kind of math they're teaching in school is very different from Kumon, and yet both children are way ahead in the school program, so there must be some solid value to the basics they're learning in Kumon. I think Kumon has given both of them a grasp of the basics which has allowed them to flourish in math.

—James Tarkington, father, California

I did everything I'm doing in school math now a year ago in Kumon. I have no problems in school. I learn new ways to solve problems in school, that's all... I never worry about math tests in school. I always finish tests early, then I check over my work.

—Billy Farlow, 11, Seattle

Every Child An Achiever

A Parent's Guide to the Kumon Method

DAVID W. RUSSELL

INTERCULTURAL GROUP

New York and Tokyo

Intercultural Group, Inc.
10 East 23rd Street, #600
New York, NY 10010

First Edition
ISBN: 1-881267-09-1

Contents

Acknowledgments

My only problem in writing this book has been not having enough room to include comments from all the people—especially the children—who made such a strong impression on me. So many kids asked, "Am I going to be in the book?" and I wanted to promise each of them a cameo, but that just isn't possible. I can only say thank you to all the children and all the parents who helped me to understand Kumon better. I want to give special thanks to Dean, Tom, and Lynda in Toronto, Matt in Cincinnati, Shinichiro Iwasaki in New Jersey, Tatsuo Miyakoshi in Osaka, Craig Sherman, whose writings on Kumon, shared with me by the Kumon staff, I gratefully acknowledge, and, most especially, to Mr. Toru Kumon himself for making this book possible.

D.R.

Kumon's Spectacular Growth
Total Worldwide Students

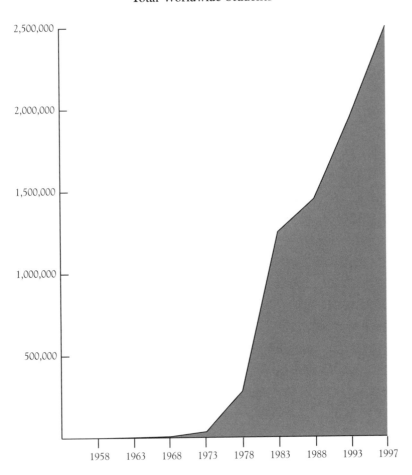

Data: Kumon Institute Education 09/97

The "Kumon Miracle"

I n its June 4, 1990 issue, *Time* magazine ran an article entitled "Mathematics Made Easy." In just a few paragraphs it described a radical new import from Japan, a kind of educational system for teaching math that was sweeping across North America. Not a super high-tech approach using computers or laser-driven optical disc readers, but a familiar, and in some ways even old-fashioned approach to math teaching that our grandparents would have recognized: drills and more drills, endless rows of calculations, and daily homework. No calculators, no computers, and no artificial intelligence. Just pencil and paper and calculations done in each student's head. No credit for problems that are almost correct—hand in a perfect paper or do it again.

The *Time* article was even more puzzling for not criticizing this very traditional approach to education. It quoted people like Ilene Black, vice principal of the Sumiton (Alabama) Elementary School, the first of nearly 200 American schools to have adopted Kumon at that point:

"One of the first things our teachers noticed was the change in attitude of the students. The parents are very positive; they love the fact that their children like it; they don't have to make them do their homework." The principal of a Texas elementary school added: "This program has helped to give them (the students in Kumon) self-confidence, a better self-image and motivation."

Kids who like to do homework, who feel more motivated and have a greater sense of self-image—to many readers it must have sounded like a dream. For many others it must have struck a very loud chord, because over 3,000 people wrote or called Kumon as a result of that one article. Kumon's regional office in Houston had to put in extra phone lines to handle all the incoming calls. Similar articles in *Newsweek* and *The Wall Street Journal* were equally flattering and equally effective in stirring up interest in this learning method they referred to as Kumon. Clearly, a lot of parents were not satisfied with how their children were doing in school and wanted something more.

Although Kumon did (and apparently still does) very little advertising, the word spread quickly from one parent to another. Today there are privately-run Kumon educational centers from coast to coast, in-school programs in numerous states, and special adult education programs operating in major corporations such as Texas Instruments and Johnson & Johnson's subsidiary, Vistakon.

What's going on? Why are parents from L.A. to Portland, Maine, from Houston to Toronto, Canada rushing to enroll

As Kumon spreads throughout North America, many companies are considering the Kumon Method for their in-house employee training programs. One good example of Kumon in action is Texas Instruments, where instructor David Beal uses the Kumon Method to help employees extend their skills. With a better grasp of the basics, many employees will find increased opportunities for advancement.

their children to study extra math, do extra homework and take extra tests? What is Kumon and why is it so popular?

Such questions did not even occur to me until 1992, for I had lived my life in blissful ignorance of modern methods in education until that time. Having become a father only two years before, I knew that sooner or later I would have to come to grips with various choices in schooling. And as our son passed his second birthday, my wife—who is more in-tune with these matters than I—was already strongly hinting that it was time for us to begin thinking about our child's education. "Within the next year or two we should put him in a good pre-school program," she said, "The younger the child, the easier it is for him to learn." From what I had already seen of my own child, I was aware that children can absorb a tremendous amount at an early age. And I had always known from my own educational experience that if the teacher is good, learning becomes fun not work. At first, somewhat unprepared to respond to my wife's question, I half-heartedly joked: "Yes, but couldn't we wait a little while to discuss this, like until after he's graduated from college?"

Fortunately, the Russell household's entire discussion of education was left pending—though not for long—when a whole new world of educational possibilities was opened up to this father by a single question asked of me in a telephone call from New York.

I should explain that phone calls from New York City are not everyday events in my home. I live in Tokyo, where I have worked as a professional writer and editor for over a decade. I learned to read and speak Japanese in college, after which I decided to live and work in Japan. Since then I have specialized in writing about Japanese cultural matters, business, politics, and society.

Far from examining Japanese educational methods, I have often worked as an investigative journalist covering everything from corporate takeovers to the keiretsu industrial groups. Although as a parent with a young child, I am naturally interested in educational opportunities and options, I am not, by any stretch of the imagination, an expert on Japanese education. For this reason, I was surprised when my agent in New York called to ask: "How would you like to research the Kumon educational program both in Japan and in the United States and Canada, and then write a book about what you discover?" He continued, saying, "There's very little available in English about it." I had, of course, heard the name—it's hard to live in Japan and not hear about Kumon, especially if you have a child. You're bound to see Kumon toys in the stores. And in fact, all I could say to him for certain about Kumon was that they made some neat little jigsaw puzzles that my two year-old loves to play with. To which he replied, "Exactly, that's why you should do the book. You have no real prior knowledge of the subject, you're neither pro nor con, and you can do research in Japanese as well as English. A publisher here in New York is interested in doing the book, and I think you're the writer for the job. What do you say?"

"I don't know what to say."

"Say yes."

A few weeks later I found myself in a very modern office building in central Tokyo, sitting in a room with several Kumon executives. I explained the purpose of my research and they were very cooperative. In fact, everyone was so nice that I began to wonder if I was in for the classic corporate snow job—lots of attractive company brochures, smiley PR people, but no opportunity to find out what the Kumon Method is really all about. To my surprise, Kumon was just the opposite. Half an hour after our first meeting one of the managers put me on a local train and took me across Tokyo to a Kumon center in a nearby suburb. There I found a single large, colorfully-decorated room with several long tables, lots of chairs, and three women preparing for the day's work.

Even as one of the women came forward to introduce herself as the instructor, the front door opened and three bubbly, kindergarten-age kids came bounding into the room.

They ran over to talk to one of the assistants in the back, and, in just a minute, mothers started appearing at the door with more children. Soon the room was full of bouncing, chattering, very normal-looking three-and four-year-olds. And then, as if responding to some signal invisible to me, they all took out what looked to me like little workbooks (I later learned that they were actually packets of worksheets) from a box of files, sat down in groups around the room, picked up pencils, and went to work. I would be exaggerating to say that the room was completely silent. But I know how hard it is for a young child to keep quiet for two minutes and concentrate on anything. Here was a whole room-

ful of kids working seriously, occasionally laughing, saying
something to a friend nearby, but generally absorbed in
what they were doing for the next ten or fifteen minutes. I
talked to the instructor for some time and nothing in the
room changed. I was convinced that whatever was in those
workbooks must have been very interesting because not a
lot of heads came up in that time.

After just this one visit, I had to admit, I was interested.
Later on, the people at the Kumon office in Tokyo (their
head office is in Osaka, Japan which I visited later) satisfied
some of my curiosity by showing me the various levels of
worksheets and explaining how their system works. On my
first visit to Osaka, I was introduced to Mr. Toru Kumon,
founder and chairman of the Kumon Institute of Education.
We had a chance to talk at length about the methods and
system he had devised. At that time, I told Mr. Kumon that
what I really wanted to do was to visit Kumon centers in
North America. I wanted to see with my own eyes how the
Kumon Method works with children in the United States
and Canada. I wanted to talk to parents and instructors and
lots of kids. With all due respect to Mr. Kumon, I knew that
I would learn more about the Kumon system in North
America from what parents, students, and instructors had to
tell me than from reading a lot of books in Tokyo, and I told
him so. He surprised me by agreeing wholeheartedly. He
told me that this was the best way to see Kumon in action
and urged me to visit as many centers as possible. "Talk to
the children," he said with a cryptic smile. I didn't understand what the smile meant, but I knew that I wanted to

talk to a lot of children. We shook hands and he wished me good luck.

My discussion with Mr. Kumon was followed by a trip around much of North America. I visited dozens of Kumon centers in a variety of settings, met with many instructors, scores of parents, and hundreds of happy, excited, interesting kids. I found that all of them were delighted to talk about Kumon and what it meant to them personally.

What follows here is my own story. It includes comments from parents and kids, as well as from Kumon instructors and excerpts from Kumon's literature when I felt that they had captured the essence of some point better than I could. It is both what I have learned and what I have come to understand based on my experience. This book has come to be my own personal way of explaining what Kumon is all about.

Every Child An Achiever

A Parent's Guide to the Kumon Method

Chapter 1

What Is Kumon?

The teaching method called Kumon, as I soon discovered, is a simple, methodical approach to learning. Although the Kumon Method has been applied to other subjects, it was originally designed to teach math, and, to date, the most common application is still in teaching mathematics. For this reason, we often hear it called "Kumon math." In fact, the Kumon Method is also being applied in Japan, for example, to the teaching of the English, French, German and Japanese languages. (As of this writing the Kumon reading program in English is not yet available at every center in North America, while the Kumon math program is taught in every Kumon center. And since it is the math program that currently attracts the largest number of parents to Kumon, I will refer only to math instruction in this book.)

It is important to note that the ultimate purpose of the Kumon Method is not simply to develop superior academic skills, such as math skills. Although it is demonstrably effec-

1

tive at teaching mathematics, the real purpose of Kumon is to provide an effective means to develop the untapped potential of each and every child.

Stop. Maybe you'd better read that again. If it sounds a little too grandiose to you, I'm not surprised. Though I see it in a different light today, I felt the same way when I first heard it. In fact, at the start, I pretty much ignored such comments in the Kumon literature, thinking that all this talk about "developing every child's innate potential" is just advertising double-talk. What I have come to realize is that the Kumon people are very serious about this.

If you were to read some of founder Toru Kumon's writings, you would find at least as much general philosophy as anything else. Mr. Kumon, who started the method that bears his name 35 years ago, is a devout believer in the potential of children. Not just gifted children, but underprivileged children, handicapped children, children with learning disabilities, virtually any child. Thus, when Mr. Kumon writes about education he very seldom writes specifically about math. Instead, he talks a lot about children and about their tremendous potential to develop.

His tone is almost reverential when he writes about the power of children, even of very young children, to learn and to grow. In Japan, very few educators have as much acknowledged success, much less the experience on which to base such comments. When he finally does use math as an example, such as mentioning how many pre-school children have learned to solve algebraic equations, he does not appear to be bragging about how far he has guided young

minds into the realm of mathematics. (That seems of relatively little interest to him.) Instead, he is pointing to the
fantastic abilities of young minds to absorb, to understand,
and to skillfully make use of complex information. Whether
a four-year-old has learned to do algebra or read Japanese
characters, he feels, is of less concern than the fact that the
child has demonstrated once again that our adult preconceptions about the human mind are pitifully inadequate.

Some observers have commented on the Kumon
Method, saying that training a child to do such things is not
impossible. "What is the practical advantage," they ask, "in
training four-year-olds to use algebra." Toru Kumon has
replied that a child who has begun to learn mathematics or
reading or music has become aware of his or her ability to
learn and will almost surely expand that learning with each
passing year. Moreover, during my own discussions with parents and instructors, I discovered that most share this belief.
And they feel that those children who have learned
through the Kumon Method have acquired more than
knowledge, they have also learned concentration and developed both good study skills and an ability to learn on their
own. Even so, during my discussions with Kumon instructors, I also discovered that some parents misunderstand the
purpose of the program. Some ask why any parent would
want to turn their child into a math whiz. Kumon's reply to
this question is that their goal is not to produce a math
whiz, but to use math (or any other subject) as a means to
get the child "hooked" on the excitement of learning. In
Kumon's experience, young children who are able to do

high school level math are invariably children who like to read. Within only a few years they almost always demonstrate excellence in a number of other areas as well.

The belief at Kumon is that children who can handle higher math at an early age will become outstanding all-around students later on. And they have had thirty-five years of experience teaching children and watching them grow. The Kumon Institute of Education was founded in Japan in 1958 with a few hundred students. Over the next thirty-five years it grew rapidly as literally millions of Japanese families decided that Kumon was the right method for their children. Although Kumon does not advertise the fact, it is no coincidence that at the very time the program was growing in Japan, international test comparisons indicated that Japanese students consistently excelled in areas such as mathematics, in every case far outperforming children in North America and Europe. It was not long before the "secret" of the Kumon Method spread. Kumon centers began to spring up around the world in the late 1970s and 1980s. Today there are about 21,000 Kumon centers worldwide providing lessons to approximately two million students every week. Altogether, Toru Kumon's home-crafted approach to learning has already reached roughly 9 million students, and with the current rate of growth that number will double before very long.

The Kumon Philosophy

One thing is obvious about Toru Kumon. He is crazy—crazy about children, that is. "The most important thing in the world," he told me, "is to open up new worlds for our children to explore." He believes that every child possesses a vast, untapped potential to learn. In his words: "Every child is a 'gifted' child in ways we normally do not appreciate." And his evidence supports that assumption. From Toru Kumon's experience, this has proven to be just as true to form if the child comes from a poor family or a wealthy family, is physically handicapped or an athletic superstar, lives in an urban ghetto or on a farm in the country. Every child has the potential to learn far beyond his or her parents' expectations. It is our job as educators, Kumon says, not to stuff knowledge into children as if they were merely empty boxes, but to encourage each individual child to want to learn, to enjoy learning and to be capable of studying whatever they need to or wish to in the future.

From the Kumon point of view, educators should help children discover the sense of pride, satisfaction, and confidence that comes with studying something difficult and then mastering it. If this sounds like an idealist talking, it certainly is—an 80 year-old idealist who has seen his ideals turn into reality thousands upon thousands of times.

Schools

If we as parents accept just a little part of Toru Kumon's idealism, we must believe in the potential of children, at least of our own children, to grow. What, then, is more vital to each of us, and by extension to the future of our world, than a school? Schools should be the most important buildings in any town: clean, well-equipped, staffed by the best people available, and funded with every last dollar we can spare. Shouldn't each school be thought of as something like a temple dedicated to the future possibilities of the human race?

Yet some educators and many parents complain that schools in the real world are often just the opposite. In our inner cities many have become little more than day-care centers, and even in some well-to-do suburbs, schools are under tremendous pressure to pay for good teachers and state-of-the-art facilities.

A lot of Kumon people tell us that Kumon is supposed to supplement the school math program. I don't believe it. I think the school math program supplements Kumon, because I know our school just isn't teaching the basics of math any more.

—Public school teacher, Massachusetts

From tight budgets to the continuing spread of drugs and violence, schools all over the world face an array of problems. Sadly, even the best educators find themselves limited by the structural, economic, and political realities of the institutions in which they teach, and these same problems are faced with alarming frequency in Japan just as they are in the United States or Canada. As a result, schools do not always operate as we hope they would.

To take just a small example, consider the modern public or private school. When you walk into the school, what are you likely to see? Photos of students who became National Merit Scholars? Not likely. In most, there is a display case somewhere nearby filled with trophies from sports competitions. Last year's All-State football championship, All-County swim team, hockey team, basketball team, maybe there is even an award for setting new state records in track and field. "These are all worthy achievements," says Kumon, "but why are schools—and the communities they serve—so eager to boast of these achievements above all others?"

"Of course, sports are an essential part of a child's growth, and no school should ignore its duty to develop children's bodies as well as their minds, but," Kumon continues, "it is ten times, a hundred times more important for schools to expand the scope of our children's mental abilities than to break records in athletic events." Perhaps it is time to consider whether we currently invest too much time, money and energy in reaching less critical goals, setting less necessary records, and bringing home the less-important kind of trophies. Do we commemorate students' achievements from the past a little too much rather than celebrating their potential for changing the world in the future?

I remember well my own school days (and I'm sure every other parent has similar memories), in which academic achievement was recognized and rewarded in a very formal way, whereas nothing could compare to being a star on the football, soccer, or hockey team. Of course, sports are public, social events, and so it is easy for children to attach great importance to them. Academic excellence, on the other hand, is a very private, personal exercise. Those who excelled in my school were looked upon as "nerds." In particular, students who excelled in math were viewed as "freaks," usually with few friends and limited interests outside studying. (Secretly, I believe that most of the faculty probably preferred the sports stars to the academic stars, for the athletes were often more outgoing and cheerful.)

Of course, when I was in high school the personal computer did not exist, biotechnology was a dream, and lasers were used in laboratories, not in portable stereos at the beach. Being captain of the football team at college was probably as good a way to land a job back then as any other. Unfortunately for many of our children, those days are all but gone.

Today in the United States and Canada, just as in Japan, combined forces within government and industry are pushing for the creation of a "knowledge-based society." All worthwhile jobs in the future (meaning when our children grow up and have to go looking for jobs) will be in what we today refer to as "information intensive" or "high tech" fields. It is sometimes difficult for us as parents to realize that many of the jobs our children will someday be applying for do not yet exist. Not only will the level of their education be absolutely crucial to holding a job twenty years from now, but their ability to acquire new knowledge between now and then will be even more important to their success. In this sense, now as never before, education is so extremely vital to our children's future. Yet in many ways our schools are not preparing our children for the world they will soon face. And let me, here and now, join concerned parents everywhere who emphatically state that the blame cannot be laid at the schoolhouse door, for the simple reason that most of the budgetary and personnel problems of our schools are of our own making. Too many of our communities proudly announce that they are building the world of the future, while they provide facilities and curricula better suited to life in the past.

Worse yet, even as we move inexorably towards this new, increasingly complex world, in overall comparisons with many other modern cultures, our children's test scores are sliding steadily downhill. It seems that every month some new study appears in the newspaper showing that a majority of high school students in the United States cannot find England on a map or write a coherent essay of one page. Less than half of these same high school students can write 9/100 as a decimal, and only a very small fraction can compute how much simple interest is due on a $1,000 loan for one year at 6% interest. And we wonder how our governments run up huge deficits!

It is sometimes easy to forget that only a few decades ago there were tens of thousands of jobs for unskilled workers. To believe that these jobs will always be there is nothing short of self-deception, for we already know that they are disappearing rapidly. As industries continue to automate and invest in new equipment, workers are being forced to retrain and to learn the skills necessary to operate increasingly-sophisticated production equipment.

A decade or more from now, when today's children are grown, "unskilled" labor will refer to people who can only operate equipment designed in the 1990s. An eight year-old child today, applying for the equivalent of a secretarial job at age twenty, will have to be able to read and understand the manual for an integrated office computer system that does not even exist today. If that same child studies adequately from now on in an educational environment that stimulates learning, understanding that manual will not be a problem. If our children learn the basics of reading, mathematics, science and other essential fields, they should be prepared for whatever challenges the future may bring. If they don't study, or if the educational system—for whatever reason—allows them to graduate without learning essential information, we as parents will find that millions of normal, intelligent children cannot land or hold worthwhile jobs in the future.

The Kumon path to knowledge

Most schools provide study materials to their students on what could be referred to as a "least common denominator" basis. That is to say, a majority of children in any class should be able to finish a certain textbook by a certain grade level. Some may find it easy and some may find it difficult, but if everyone gets through Book Five by the end of Grade Five, at least they have all, in theory, acquired a certain minimum level of knowledge. This attitude was certainly evident when I went to school, and probably was the same for you and your parents. In some schools today, children who are more "advanced" are permitted to study ahead of their normal grade level; those children who are considered "slower" are given remedial help. Thus, instead of keeping all the students together in one group they may, in some progressive schools, be divided into two or three groups. However, because of ever-increasing class size and the considerable burden placed on most teachers to keep things moving at a certain pace, truly personalized, individual instruction is very rare.

And perhaps most important of all, the educational process is still directed by an adult—the teacher. Because learning is teacher-driven in the typical educational system, children all too easily become passive agents in the learning process.

I'm very impressed with how everything in the teaching materials interlocks. In school, teachers seem to jump around from topic to topic, but I have to say I like the solid progression in Kumon. To me the most important thing is to make sure my daughter has a solid foundation in her studies. In her school, I know there are too many kids in each class, and even the advanced classes are growing bigger. The teachers have to keep moving from one lesson to the next, plus watch over a roomful of rowdy kids. It's not easy. I think too many kids can fall through the cracks too easily. That sure doesn't happen with Kumon.

                            —Jennifer Krieger, mother, Indiana

The Kumon Method turns the process upside-down. The goal of Kumon is to make learning a student-driven activity, to put the responsibility for learning on the learner, not on the teacher. It is a fair question to ask why Kumon has adopted such an unusual method. The answer, according to the Kumon Institute, is that decades of experience with tens of thousands of children has shown that learning occurs most efficiently when two criteria are met:

1) the level of the material to be learned corresponds exactly to the learner's level of ability

2) the rate of progress is controlled by the student, not the teacher.

Thus, the Kumon philosophy holds, if all students study at exactly the appropriate level, they are much less likely to become discouraged, and so will much more easily develop an interest in and enthusiasm for learning. The more they learn, the more they want to learn. Because the children set their own pace, there is no pressure whatsoever to compete, and children discover that they want to do more because they enjoy what they are doing. As they develop other skills along the way, they begin to blossom, to grow towards their full potential.

Perhaps the idea that children will learn to enjoy

studying causes some parents to smile and say to themselves, "Well, maybe other people's children, but not mine…" Fear not, for while I enjoyed reading about the Kumon philosophy, I was equally skeptical that it really works in practice. As I discovered from conducting hundreds of parent/child interviews (and as you will see from some of the quotes I have included here), it not only works exactly as Kumon claims, it works better than most parents would have believed possible. The term "Kumon miracle" did not originate from Kumon, but from the parents of Kumon students themselves.

Kumon aims to provide each child with a course of instruction that best meets his or her individual needs. This does not mean that the learning materials are custom-designed for each child; that is not possible.

What Kumon gives to each child is a meticulously-researched and refined path which can enable any student to climb from the most elementary basics up to the most advanced heights of a particular field of study. The Kumon philosophy says that there is a natural sequence in learning many subjects (especially math) and that study should follow this order. Learning should proceed like a single path up a tall mountain, but the steps should be short and the trail not so difficult in any one spot that students will become discouraged and give up. Sometimes after a difficult patch, the student should be able to relax, to walk on a plateau for a bit, gather energy and confidence before starting up the next incline.

The Kumon path is composed of thousands of small

steps that guide students forward little by little. The steps are the same for every student, but every child climbs his or her own individual path. There is no class to worry about, no pressure to keep up with anyone. This allows children to proceed at their own pace from beginning to end.

Because the steps are small, children feel totally confident in moving from one to the next; there is never a missed step. And, because the incline varies constantly, but not suddenly, they are always being challenged by new material, yet never forced to learn things that are too difficult.

On reaching their level, Kumon students are allowed to rest (by doing work that they are comfortable with), and then they are challenged by slightly more difficult work again. In this way they are always able to absorb what they have learned and are always stimulated to go a little further. The Kumon philosophy, however, is to never put pressure on any student to advance. Only when a student has demonstrated complete mastery of the previous step is it time to move up to the next one. Thus, no student ever advances even the smallest step without having a rock-solid foundation for support. In climbing the Kumon path, the goal is not to reach for the top of the mountain, nor even to climb there quickly. The real goal is to advance step by step without any gaps in learning, to feel completely confident about what you know and what you can do. How fast and how far one climbs is entirely up to each individual.

In Kumon, the written materials (referred to as worksheets) take each child along this path independently, and the instructor supplements the materials only when needed. While each student must successfully complete the same materials, each child is working at his or her own pace, and so each is at a different point in the program. When a child wants input from the instructor the response is always personal, because it is geared to exactly what that child is studying.

When a student in any level from 3A through K completes all 200 worksheets in that level, an achievement test follows. These tests consist of problems that use the skills developed in the previous level, as well as a few problems that draw upon skills learned earlier. In this way each student has opportunities to review and reinforce the building blocks of math and also to identify any points that might not be as strong as they were a few months ago. Like all Kumon work, these tests are designed to be completed within a specific time range.

Needless to say, this approach to education is a big change from what most children are used to in school. The primary function of Kumon's approach is to provide the most efficient, most individually satisfying learning system possible. As it turns out, this very approach to learning becomes a form of education in itself.

Children soon discover that learning requires personal effort and that no one else can make that effort for you: Mom and Dad can't do it, the instructor can't do it, and your friends can't do it. Either you work hard and produce results that you can be proud of, or you don't.

I spoke with many parents who felt that, for whatever

A wonderful thing about Kumon is that it instills in students the feeling that they've got to be responsible for their own work. Rather than expecting someone to spoon-feed them everything, they have to take over the learning process themselves and determine when they need to ask for assistance and when they don't. Kumon makes children feel they're responsible for their own education, and they respond to that in a very positive way.

—Lynda Montis, instructor, Toronto

reason, this basic idea seems to have been lost over the years in the school system. As one instructor commented, "In Kumon the child learns very early that he gets out of it only what he puts into it. That comes as a shock for some of today's kids. There is no free lunch in Kumon. Nobody gets moved up to the next level simply because the class is moving up to the next grade. It's a very basic lesson in taking responsibility for one's own achievements, and I'm happy to say that children respond to it very well."

Kumon math

The principles of the Kumon math program are very simple. The program begins with the assumption that all children (and adults) need to know a certain amount of math. For children, this is more than a matter of being able to tell time or count change in a store. Our children will be tested and tested again as they proceed through elementary school, junior high school, high school, and into college. Specific math skills are required to pass these tests and to advance along the educational ladder. In other words, children must not only learn math in a general, practical sense, but must be able to attain certain standardized target levels of achievement.

The Kumon system helps children to move smoothly up that educational ladder, learning all the basics of each step along the way, learning to work with this information quickly and easily, and learning it all thoroughly, so that it is never intimidating. Thus, the child acquires not merely knowledge and skill, but also confidence.

Kumon does not use a text book. Thus, there are no changing "math fashions" in Kumon. Instead, each child follows a carefully sequenced series of short, manageable worksheets (there are over 4,000 in the entire program). These worksheets introduce new concepts, demonstrate problem-solving techniques, and most of all, provide a deep, solid foundation of practice and repetition for each level of study. The students must attain a required level of competence at each level—both in terms of accuracy and completion time—in order to progress to the next level.

Accuracy is emphasized because that is what math is all about. Unlike, history, for example, basic mathematics is not open to interpretation. In the kind of problems that students encounter, there are only correct answers and all other answers. Kumon stresses the need to arrive at the correct answer every time (although there are often multiple ways to obtain that answer). "Sort of" knowing something is not good enough in Kumon. A child who "sort of" understands fractions does not really understand them.

Speed is also emphasized, not in a fanatical way, but in a practical way. If a child understands the concepts that he or she is working with, a worksheet can be completed in a short time, and done perfectly. If not, then the student needs more practice. When the child has really mastered a concept and retains the knowledge of earlier lessons as well, it is time to move on to something new.

This is a very simple system. The way to advance in

math is to proceed to the next level of difficulty only when you have completely grasped the previous one. And the way to determine if a student has mastered any level is to monitor accuracy and speed. Typically, a child will repeat the same level several times until a desired degree of accuracy is attained and, if necessary, repeat it again several more times to be able to complete the exercises in the prescribed time range.

Standard Completion Time

While insisting on accuracy in math is not unusual, Kumon's emphasis on a certain degree of speed in completing the worksheets is one of the features that sets it apart from many other educational programs. For that reason, and also because I found that this element of the Kumon Method is often misunderstood, I want to discuss it here and at greater length later on.

In Kumon, the target times toward which students are working are referred to as standard completion times or SCTs. The SCT is the interval within which a student must complete a given worksheet, including time required to correct mistakes. There is a designated SCT range for every worksheet in each of the twenty sub-levels (or "sets") within the twenty-one levels of Kumon math. Each of these sets contains ten worksheets.

When a student can answer all the problems in one of these sets correctly, and is able to do so within a reasonable period of time, it is clear that he or she is ready to

There's no point in rushing a kid to finish quickly if he's going to get a lot of problems wrong. But if you learn the stuff well in the first place and then you learn to do it fast, that's really helpful... Kumon has really helped with my math.

—John Liu, 10, San Francisco

take a small step up to the next set. The SCT is not used at all for the very first level (currently 5A), but is introduced in the next level, where many young children would start. The SCTs for these early levels run from half a minute to two minutes per worksheet. Beginning with Level B, as the problems become more difficult, the SCTs naturally become longer, rising to between three and five minutes, then from five to seven minutes, and in the very highest levels (per-mutations, combinations, probability and statistics), from thirty to sixty minutes for a single worksheet.

The SCTs are based on years of experience with many students doing the same work. Not a few hundred or a few thousand students, but literally tens of thousands of children worldwide. These times reflect average completion times for students who have successfully mastered the material involved at each sub-level, and they have been refined again and again to make them more realistic. SCTs are not designed to be too easy or too difficult. They are practical guidelines which force students to concentrate on their work while still achieving accuracy. Needless to say, these abilities prove extremely useful throughout the child's edu-cational experience.

In this way, the basis of the Kumon approach is true "child-centered" learning. Each child progresses at his or her own pace, not driven by a need to reach a certain point in a textbook by a certain week. Each child advances naturally, at a comfortable pace, but along a prescribed course designed to meet university math requirements. Some chil-dren will naturally move through the Kumon system faster

or slower than others, but this makes no difference whatsoever. The point is for each child to advance properly. And
that is done only by learning everything in step one before
going to step two, and so on. It is not a race. There are no
prizes for finishing a Kumon grade level faster than anyone
else. Because there is no pressure to keep up with anyone
else, nor to score higher than anyone else on a test, each
child is allowed to develop, to grow, and to advance individually. The only fundamental targets at every step of the
Kumon system are accuracy and speed, and even in these
areas there is no pressure. As mathematical skills are
acquired, each child naturally develops the ability to solve
problems quickly and without mistakes. One common com-
plaint that I heard from parents was that their children had
been advanced through their elementary—and sometimes
even junior high school education—without truly understanding the fundamentals of certain subjects. As any
Kumon instructor can tell you, math is one subject where
any gap in understanding is not merely a bit of missing
information, but an essential part out of the puzzle of
higher learning. When students do not really understand
part of their math education, they are aware of it, and
this makes them uncomfortable. Math class becomes something they would rather avoid. (How many parents can
remember the same feelings? Did you—as I did—ever come
up with little strategies to avoid being called on in class?)
But no matter how well children avoid participating, there
are always tests, and test-taking can become a terror from
which there is no escape.

A fundamental tenet of Kumon's is the belief that children must learn math from the basics and must learn it completely. Only then will they feel comfortable, confident, and relaxed, and only in that frame of mind will they learn as they were meant to.

Chapter 2

History

Toru Kumon admits he was a lazy, good-for-nothing student when he was young. "My favorite activity was lying around the house," he remarked during our discussion. In the early 1920s, at the age of 12, he was thrust into a new private school, one dedicated to a principle called *jigaku-jishuu* ("self-study, self-learning"). In his new math class, for example, the teacher did not stand at the blackboard and lecture, as did all other teachers young Toru had previously encountered. Instead, the teacher instructed the students to work on their own at their desks, going through the prescribed textbook at whatever pace felt comfortable. If they had a question about anything they read, they could ask the teacher and get a clear explanation. Kumon took to this system like a fish to water: "It suited me perfectly. I didn't want to be a great math student, but I did want to get far enough ahead so that I could take it easy. Also, I hated having teachers breathing down my neck, telling me what to do and giving lectures all the time."

Under this new, self-motivated system Toru Kumon progressed rapidly. When he reached equations on his own, he recalls thinking, "Hey, this is fun. Why didn't they teach interesting stuff like this while we were in elementary school?" He recounted how he had zipped through the program, and had finished junior high math a year early. For senior high school, he returned to a regular high school; it felt constricting. He remembers looking around at the other students: a few bright ones followed the teacher's lessons perfectly, a large bunch in the middle sort of understood what was going on, but never really seemed like they were on solid ground because the class kept moving along so fast, and a small group at the other end of the spectrum always seemed to be lost, just struggling to keep up with what was going on day to day. How inefficient, he thought, and what a waste of time and effort for the majority of kids who need more time to really understand the textbook. And what a strain on the more advanced kids who must keep from getting too far ahead and losing the rest of the class.

Toru Kumon went on to study math in a nationally famous university and became a math teacher in both public and private high schools afterwards. As the years passed, he never forgot his days of "self-study, self-learning" in that private junior high, eventually coming to the conclusion that regular schools were sadly inefficient. Worse yet, what they were wasting wasn't simply time, but the learning power of all the young minds that passed through their doors. Then as now, however, there was little that one teacher could do to change an entire nationwide system.

Kumon simply did his best to work within the system and to teach his students that mathematics can be interesting.

Years passed, and he continued to teach in the public schools. Then one day something happened that changed the course of his life. Kumon tells the story this way:

It all started with a test paper.

One day my wife came into my study carrying a sheet of paper. It was a math test that my son Takeshi (who was then in the second grade) had taken. He had received a poor mark, which was unusual for him, but I didn't think anything of it. However, my wife seemed quite concerned.

'Is it all right to let him get marks like this? Don't you think we should teach him at home?,' she asked in a worried tone of voice.

At the time, I had been teaching high school math for twenty years, and frankly, it had never occurred to me to teach my own son math from the time he was in elementary school. What was the point?

'One bad mark is nothing to panic over. In the first place, I have no idea what or how to teach an elementary school child. As soon as he gets to junior high school I'll start teaching him a few things,' I answered, hoping to persuade her not to make such a fuss.

But my wife would not accept this. 'Can you guarantee that he'll be all right if you wait until he gets to junior high school?,' she asked. I didn't know what to

Toru Kumon continues to refine the Kumon Method, to share
the fruits of his knowledge with parents and teachers worldwide,
and to help children to enjoy learning.

answer. She went on, 'You love teaching other people's children, and you work hard at it. Surely you would find it even more rewarding to teach your own son.'

When she becomes insistent like this about something, there's no point in arguing, I thought. I decided I might as well give it a try. How difficult could it be to teach a second grader?

The first thing I did was to examine the second grade arithmetic textbooks used in schools across the nation. I was surprised to find that, in some parts, I did not immediately understand them. Maybe it was because they were different from the textbooks I had used when I was young, but simply opening them up and reading left me puzzled. When I went back and read them from the beginning they made sense. Yet when I looked at all of this from the point of view of a high school math teacher, there seemed to be many things that were unnecessary for advancing to the higher grades of math. 'Who prepared such a disorganized texts?,' I wondered.

You see, if elementary school arithmetic is to lead to high school mathematics, it must follow a certain logical order. I felt that the unnecessary parts should all be deleted and the order of presentation of the remaining material should be rearranged.

I decided that the school textbook was not the best way to proceed. So I bought one of the commercially available math drill books and started Takeshi working with that.

After only a short time I discovered that he was taking too much time to do things that were not particularly important. Naturally, that was no fun for him, and he was quickly losing interest in studying. I decided that even with these drill books he was wasting his study time and not developing the enjoyment of math that I had discovered early in life. Finally, having no other choice, I decided to create my own simple materials to help my son study.

I began by examining all the elementary and junior high school math texts from a high school teacher's perspective. What material is really necessary to give a student the ability to solve high school math easily? I eliminated what I considered a waste of time and expanded the points I thought were essential. Then I considered the order of presentation. I devised a natural progression that would take Takeshi step by step from the easiest arithmetic up to the more complex math functions that I was teaching in my regular classes. As a teacher, I knew well enough that there isn't sufficient time to do adequate drill and practice in class, so I emphasized these features in the materials I began to create.

I drew up dozens and dozens of calculation problems on both sides of loose leaf paper so that Takeshi would get plenty of drill on the most important elements in math. I made him do just one sheet of paper each day. Even with all those problems, the material was so similar that if he could do one problem he should be able to do all the problems on a single sheet. As a result, he never spent more than thirty minutes a day on his new "homework." Because the material was clear and easy to follow and because the sheets I was making up could be finished very quickly, he did not develop an antagonism toward this study, but, on the contrary, grew to like it.

Each day he would do his work while my wife looked on, and then at night when I came home, I would mark the problems he had answered incorrectly. By seeing where he was having difficulty, I was able to make small adjustments on the next day's assignment.

The next day he would begin by correctly solving on his own the problems I had marked as having wrong answers. Then he would do the sheet assigned for that day. He continued to study like this, and I continued to create new "homework" for a few years. Still, he never spent more than half an hour on any one assignment and often much less.

By the time he was in sixth grade he had completed the differential and integral calculus of the high school curriculum. I tried giving him a few college entrance examination problems and he was able to solve most of them with ease. I remember how relieved I felt that if he could handle this level of work while still an elementary school student, he would have no worries about math for the rest of his school life and need never fear the college entrance examinations.

Toru Kumon discovered at home the tremendous advantages of the "worksheets" he was creating. His son was learning at his own pace, for he could always go back and re-do sections he didn't understand completely, and the materials he was working on were designed to carry him steadily, step by step upwards toward higher level math. And yet, the work itself seemed painless, no more than 30 minutes a day. His son recognized his own progress, and, as a result, became motivated to advance even further. He learned the pleasure of self-study, of not being compared to anyone else in a classroom or a grade level.

The first worksheets were created in 1954. Only a year or so later it was obvious that Takeshi was learning better than he ever had in school. Within another year Kumon's wife persuaded him to allow other children in the neighborhood to use the same worksheets he had developed for his own son. The results were much the same. In 1958, the Kumon Institute of Education was established in Osaka. In that first year it attracted a total of 300 students just through the recommendations of parents whose children had improved by following Kumon's teaching method. The Kumon Institute was not a school, not a substitute for the public school system, but an adjunct to it. Kumon provided a specialized program in mathematics that seemed to work for students of all ages and all levels of ability.

In no time the word spread beyond the city of Osaka. Only five years after setting up the company, the Kumon Institute had to open an office in Tokyo, and new Kumon franchise "centers" sprang up all over Japan. Although there are dozens of famous after-school education programs in Japan, Kumon became the nation's No. 1 private educational program, with approximately 1.6 million students enrolled.

Just a decade after opening in Tokyo, the first Kumon center opened in New York and a few years later a center opened in California. Thanks mostly to word-of-mouth recommendations from satisfied parents and interested teachers, the Kumon message spread across the United States and Canada. The Kumon Institute opened new centers in a host of other countries, including England, France, Germany, Switzerland, Austria, Belgium, Italy, Hong Kong, Taiwan, South Korea, Singapore, and Australia.

Less than forty years after a modest, high school math teacher designed some simple worksheets to help his own son overcome his fear of math and become a better student, Kumon has become not only the largest private instruction company in both Japan and North America, but the largest private educational institute in the world. And it is still growing.

It is interesting—and perhaps a sign of the times—that Kumon is not limited to classrooms or young students. Leading U. S. companies such as Johnson & Johnson subsidiary, Vistakon, and high-tech pioneer Texas Instruments have been implementing Kumon study programs for their employees, and report noticeable positive results among those employees who follow the program diligently. Other corporations are reported to be considering the Kumon Method as a proven and cost-effective way to increase their work forces' skill levels. There are already indications that Kumon programs will also be adopted in a number of industries. As word spreads about Kumon, its potential for use in adult education is generating considerable interest.

Toru Kumon is still active in further developing the program that he created. He has authored more than twenty books and visited many countries to lecture about the Kumon Method. His son Takeshi gave up a career at one of Japan's top securities firms to return to the family business that he had helped to inspire; today he is the president of the Kumon Institute of Education.

Chapter 3

How Does Kumon Work?

So, let's say you've heard about Kumon from a friend or neighbor, or perhaps you've read about it in the newspaper. It sounds interesting, but you're not going to make a decision about something as important as your child's education just on that basis. If you feel the same way I did, you want to talk to someone who really knows about Kumon and perhaps see it in action. At every Kumon center I visited, I found parents looking for first-hand information about the essential building blocks of the program. One example of what they learned concerned the entry procedure. Before you can even put your child into Kumon, the center will want to administer a brief placement test. It is just a means to determine where the most effective point to start your child in the program would be.

Like other parents, you will be surprised, even shocked perhaps, when the instructor tells you at what level your child will begin to study Kumon. Many a parent said to me that their child was already doing more complex work in school, but that Kumon had required the child to start at a much simpler point. The reason for this is that in the Kumon program it is absolutely essential to start each child at a skill level that is easier than what that child is already studying in school. This is nothing more than an attempt to guarantee that every child feels comfortable with the level of material right from the first worksheet. If a child finds the starting level a little too easy, that's fine; the super-easy work will pass quickly. Many parents find that they are thankful for this time because it makes it easier to acclimate their children to the routine of daily homework. If the first level or so is easy, not only are the children less likely to resist doing the homework every day, but most are happy to be achieving 100% correct answers on every worksheet right from the start.

The Kumon classrooms I visited never failed to impress me. I always find them interesting, especially when there are groups of kids inside concentrating on their worksheets. As one parent said, "It's so quiet sometimes it's kind of eerie." If you visit a Kumon center, ask how often it is open. Also ask to see some of the worksheets. And talk to the instructor at length, as well as some of the parents who might be waiting for their own children.

Nothing is as important to the success of a child in going through the materials than a good Kumon center and a good instructor. After visiting a few dozen Kumon centers on my trip around North America, I can honestly say that I would be happy to put my son in the care of any of the instructors I met. I was curious to learn how Kumon finds such dedicated people, so at one point I asked an administrator at one of Kumon's regional offices. "We don't," he replied, "they come looking for us. Kumon attracts a certain kind of person, and frankly, we're glad it does."

Placement test

One of the greatest strengths of the Kumon Method is the emphasis it places on matching the materials to the individual's abilities. In order to get started at just the right spot among roughly 4,000 worksheets, it is necessary to test each student carefully. Based on the results of the placement test (sometimes referred to as a diagnostic test), an instructor can determine exactly where to start any incoming student in order to help him or her to achieve maximum results.

Some parents feel this test is a waste of time. They feel their children should start right where they are in their school classes—especially if they're getting good grades already—and go on from there. It is true that some of these children may know multiplication or division or whatever inside-out, and they may know all the basic operations that precede it. But Kumon's point is that the mere fact that a child is doing a certain level of math in school does not guarantee that the child has attained the kind of mastery which Kumon demands in order to progress to the next level of learning.

For example, there are often cases of kids who are getting pretty good grades on multiplication tests in school, but have not really mastered addition and subtraction. The tests

Through the completely unbiased results of the placement test any child entering the Kumon system can start out at a point that is comfortable, tailored to his or her current level of knowledge, and advance smoothly from there.

are designed to bring out these "gaps" in a child's education. Thus, before entering a Kumon program, each child is tested. The tests are brief and painless. For pre-schoolers they may be little more than drawing straight lines. There are no "trick" questions. They are not designed to make any child look good or bad. The only purpose of the placement test is to determine how thoroughly a child has learned math up to this point.

The tests—as with all tests in Kumon—are timed. A student who can answer many addition problems correctly, but who needs twenty minutes to do it, has not mastered addition despite a 100% score. Thus, even among several children scoring equally on the same test it is possible to differentiate their levels of ability. In rare cases a child may finish the test in just a few minutes; obviously it was too easy and that child will be re-tested. Likewise, a very few children may spend half an hour on a test that should be completed in ten or fifteen minutes; they, too, will be given another test, but at an easier level.

It is important to remember that the purpose of the test is not to show how "fast" or "slow" a student is. The various levels of Kumon worksheets do not imply any kind of ranking. Most of all, it is important to remember that neither the placement test nor any other test in Kumon should ever be thought of as an intelligence test. Kumon does not work from the premise that this child is smart and that child is dumb. Quite the opposite—the Kumon Method assumes that every child has within him or her enormous potential to learn and to grow. The purpose of the placement test is simply to find out how much information relating to specific mathematical operations a child has already absorbed. Whether it is a little or a lot makes no difference to the process of Kumon learning. The test only indicates from what rung on the ladder a child will begin climbing. Since each child is an individual in Kumon, not a member of a class, each has his or her own ladder to climb, at his or her own pace. As I noted before, it is not a race. It is, rather, a test of self-discipline, of concentration, and effort.

Thus, if your son is ten years old and the placement test indicates that he should start at level 2A1, and your daughter is only eight, but the test results say she should start at level B1, do not worry and do not let your children worry that the little girl is "smarter" than her older brother. The test only tells you that your daughter's knowledge of basic math concepts is currently greater than her brother's. This may have nothing to do with the relative intelligence of the two children and a lot to do with their study habits, motivation, prior schooling, etc. Even after a year of Kumon exercises, if she advances four levels and he advances only two, this may be a better indicator of their attitudes towards self-study than of their intelligence.

Interestingly, Kumon is not primarily concerned with "making your children smart." The Kumon people already believe your children are smarter than you think. Their primary concern is not with raw intelligence, but rather, with ability. Intelligence is innate; ability can be enhanced and developed through effort. That is the true goal of the Kumon Method.

A comfortable starting point

Despite having said all this, and despite the assurances of Kumon instructors around the world, thousands of parents are dismayed or even shocked to discover how "low" on the scale their children are supposed to start. "Did my child fail the placement test?," some parents must be thinking. The answer is no, their child did very well. That is, they demonstrated exactly what they did and didn't understand about math. And by demonstrating their current competency level, they have indicated where they will feel comfortable entering the Kumon program. This is so important that it cannot be over-emphasized. If a child is going to enjoy math, do daily homework, come to the center twice a week, and make a serious effort to learn, he or she must feel comfortable, from the beginning of the program right to the end.

"Perhaps so," a parent might respond, "but my children are already doing work at their grade level and you want to send them backwards to work they have already done in previous grades. That's ridiculous! " The answer is no, it isn't ridiculous. Your children are not "being sent back" as some kind of punishment or insult or anything of the kind. They are being allowed to start at the point where their ability levels indicate they will feel most comfortable. If they learned addition years ago and if the placement test indicates that they know addition cold, then that's the ideal point to start working their way up through Kumon. They should find the addition problems easy and reassuring. As a

Kumon takes me step by step in math, so I feel real good about it. I had to start with addition even though I could already do multiplication and division. I think that was helpful.

—Ben Heck, 3rd grade, Virginia

result, your children will be able to do many problems quickly. They will go through that level in very little time and soon progress to the next level.

In the process, your children will develop concentration and confidence, which will provide the basis for them to advance academically. In a surprisingly short time you will find them doing work that is more advanced than what their grade-level classes are doing in school.

It must, however, come "naturally," that is, in a long series of tiny steps from a foundation where they feel totally confident. Then during the first couple of months, while your children are learning to do homework every day and getting adjusted to the Kumon program, the work will seem easy and will flow smoothly.

Dean Bradley, Development Manager in the Kumon regional office in Toronto and one of the many dedicated Kumon staff people I interviewed, stated it this way:

Kumon doesn't just use a low starting point. We use what I call a Super-Low Starting Point. Many instructors don't explain carefully enough to parents why this is necessary. We start kids at a point where we know they're going to be achievers. We can take a child who hates math, who hates anything to do with math, and start him or her at such a basic point that a single day's work takes about six minutes. You get a child doing that regularly and right away you'll see a sense of accomplishment developing. The child thinks 'I hate math, but I can do this stuff easily and I'm getting

100% right. What's the big deal?' That confidence carries him or her into the next unit and then into the next level, and before they know it, children discover that they're actually good at math. Of course, we could start every child at a higher point than we do, but for what purpose? To save a few weeks of study? It doesn't make sense. To keep the child from getting bored? A child who can knock-off his homework in a few minutes won't get bored, I assure you. And within a short time the homework will become more challenging and the child will be kept very busy. Any way you look at it, the low starting point is a critical part of the Kumon Method.

THE KUMON METHOD IN ACTION*

Each prospective student takes a
diagnostic test.

The student is enrolled in a Kumon program
at a starting point that is exactly suited
to his or her individual level
of ability.

The Kumon classroom is open two days a week.
Rather than observing a fixed schedule, each
student arranges his or her own
schedule for visiting
the classroom.

Upon entering the classroom, the student
hands in the worksheets that were assigned as
homework, which the instructor grades
and returns to be corrected, The student
corrects all the problems that have
been marked as mistakes and
eventually turns in
homework that is
100-percent
perfect.

The student receives 3 to 10 worksheets to do that day. He or she
takes a seat in the Kumon classroom (any seat), solves
the problems on the worksheets, and returns the completed
worksheets to the instructor, who notes how long it took
the student to do them, grades them, and returns
them to the student to be corrected.
The student corrects all the problems that
have been marked as mistakes and
finally returns work that is
100-percent perfect.

The student receives worksheets to do as
homework (3 to 5 worksheets
per day) and leaves.

* From a chart supplied by the Kumon Institute of Education

Classrooms

There are two general types of Kumon classroom: in-school and after-school. The first is the most familiar—the child's regular school classroom. At this writing there are 450 public and private schools in the United States that are using Kumon as part of their in-school curriculum, and many more are considering it. In-school programs are structured much like regular math programs in that a certain time is set aside every day to do Kumon worksheets. Students do their work and teachers correct it later. There is usually no homework. By and large, schools that have adopted Kumon are extremely pleased with the results (although long-term data are not yet available.) However, because schools are institutions, and institutions are sometimes slower to adopt new ideas than individual parents, the parents are often quicker to decide that they want something special for their children. As a result, a network of private Kumon "centers" has sprung up coast to coast, and more children are studying today in these centers than in the in-school programs.

Kumon learning centers might be located anywhere an instructor decides to open one. Some are held in church basements, some in community centers, and some in rented offices. The centers are usually open for Kumon two days a week and students are expected to be there twice a week. At most centers the students come whenever they please during center hours—because there is no fixed "class" there is no need for a fixed arrival time (which makes life a lot easier for parents with busy schedules.) Based on what I've

Classrooms vary, instructors vary, but the Kumon program doesn't. Kumon doesn't assign seats or set starting times. Children work at their own pace without peer pressure or teacher prompting.

seen in various centers throughout North America, an "average" Kumon day looks something like this:

Let's say you take your daughter to your local Kumon center at around 3:30 on a Thursday afternoon. Perhaps you spend a few minutes chatting with the instructor. Then you join other parents in the waiting room while your daughter enters the classroom. There she hands in her completed homework. In some centers the Kumon instructor or assistants would then mark it, in other centers you would already have marked it and your daughter would have corrected it at home. (More about this point in a moment.) In this case, let's assume the homework is marked at the center.

Your daughter then goes to a file with her name on it and takes out today's worksheets, a batch of new worksheets for homework, and homework from the previous session that has now been marked. Then she sits down to begin working. She takes any seat that is open. Again, because this is not a formal classroom, the instructor is not there to make sure that Anne Smith is sitting in Anne Smith's assigned seat. Kumon centers are very free-form, designed to reinforce the idea that learning is self-directed and that it's fun.

From this point, your child corrects any mistakes on the previous session's homework and hands in completed worksheets that are now 100% correct. If there is something she really doesn't understand and cannot correct by herself, she can always ask the instructor for help. For the most part, she discovers that her mistakes are usually careless ones and that by going over them once again she will turn up the right answer almost every time. This whole process takes only a few minutes. Then she is ready to begin today's new worksheets.

She records the time before beginning to work, then completes the appropriate number of worksheets (depending on the level of study, there are generally between three and ten sheets in a day's work.) Then, when your daughter has finished her new worksheets, she notes the time that she finishes and hands them in to be marked. Once again, she must correct the problems that she answered incorrectly. When your daughter is finished with corrections, she marks the time and results on her record sheet. The instructor looks over this record sheet and chats with her before your daughter leaves the center. You stop to say good-bye to the instructor as your daughter comes out to greet you. As you leave, you look at your watch: it's a few minutes before 4:00. Your daughter has finished today's session, she has homework to do for the next few days, and you're ready to go home, all in about thirty minutes.

In short, Kumon does not place a very great time burden on either the child or the parent. And based on the many Kumon centers I visited in North America, almost all of the parents and kids enjoy coming to the centers, talking with their peers, and generally having a good time.

Although in Japan the marking of homework is done at the centers, some parents in the United States and in Canada prefer to check their children's homework at home.

For one thing, children can see and correct their mistakes immediately, which means they have less work to do at the center. Also, because those mistakes are corrected so soon there is much less chance of continuing to repeat the same mistakes. Many parents have also reported that they like to see what their children are studying day by day. They don't have to rely on either the child or the instructor for progress reports because they know precisely how well their children are doing and where they are having trouble. Thus, there are definite merits to parental grading of homework.

Regardless of how the homework is graded, the same basic pattern of going to the center to work is repeated twice a week: hand in homework, do some worksheets, correct your mistakes, go home with new homework. Those two, roughly thirty-minute sessions, plus about twenty minutes of homework the other five nights of the week (for the days the child has not been to the center) is all there is to it. No painful schedule, no arduous late-night study, no burning the midnight oil, and not even enough time out of anyone's day to make a good excuse for not continuing with the program. Yet this very minimal time and work commitment, if done conscientiously and regularly for at least a year, produces dramatic results. I know. I've talked with hundreds of parents who would gladly get up on stage and give testimonials for what Kumon has done for their children. (One day I expect to be one of them.)

Instructors

As I have already mentioned, nothing is more important to the success of the Kumon Method than having capable instructors. Instructors not only monitor the learning process, deciding when a student is ready to move on to the next level and answering questions when a student needs help, they also provide a very special sort of reward system for each child. Many instructors say that they are surprised to find that just a few words of praise will light up a child's face. One parent in Los Angeles probably spoke for many more all across the United States and Canada when she said: "Our child thinks the world of you. Everything you say makes such a big impression, we're almost jealous."

As a result, Kumon takes great care in selecting and training instructors. Applicants who want to open their own Kumon center are carefully screened, both through written tests and interviews. Kumon also conducts a rigorous program of continuing education for its instructors, insisting that they attend special seminars and pass tests in their subject year after year.

If this sounds like undue "quality control," at Kumon they think differently. Without well-trained, dedicated instructors, the Kumon people feel that their program cannot succeed. It is no exaggeration to say that the instructors in North America must be among the most committed, diligent, hard-working educators in their respective communities. They care about students as individuals and that care shows in the results they help to achieve. Kumon is proud of

The Kumon Method attracts many excellent instructors. Dedication to their students and the ability to provide the right amount of guidance at just the right time seem to be common characteristics coast to coast.

them, as are tens of thousands of parents from coast to coast.

One interesting phenomenon that seems to be growing in the United States is that parents who originally knew nothing about the Kumon Method, become involved through their children's participation, and then find themselves becoming active in Kumon. Quite a number go on to become instructors themselves.

I knew nothing about Kumon except that it was originally a Japanese method of teaching math, and that persuaded me it was probably pretty good. My daughter was having some trouble with her math class in school, so I had her take a Kumon placement test. I looked at the materials when she was tested, and I liked them. I didn't sign her up right away. My husband and I talked about it, and two days later I enrolled her in the center. I watched her do the work, I saw what happened to her grades, her study habits and her self-confidence. About 11 months later I enrolled my son. Then I began to become more involved. I started out as a grader, and then became an assistant in the center, and then when the opportunity arose, I took the Kumon training and became an instructor myself. Right now I have a waiting list of parents who want to be assistants in my center, and some of them will probably want to become instructors someday.

—Donna Ramesh,

Kumon instructor, Ohio

Materials

At this time the worksheets are divided into a minimum of twenty-one levels in the United States and Canada; there are seven additional levels in Japan which are slowly being added to the North American program as more children progress towards the higher levels. The most elementary level is 5A, the one above that is 4A, then 3A, and so on to A, B, C and up to Level Q. Each level consists of twenty sets, each with ten worksheets. Thus, at each level there are 200 worksheets arranged in a natural order to facilitate learning.

When a new operation is introduced in Kumon, there are no lengthy pages of explanation. Instead, an example of the new principle is printed at the top of a worksheet, sometimes with a brief explanation, and a sample problem or two. The first several problems that follow are very close to the example so that students quickly build confidence in working with the new operation. In the subsequent worksheets, problems are less and less like the example, challenging students to incorporate what they have learned. This is the process that underlies the Kumon approach to teaching new concepts.

Though critics who charge that Kumon does not teach concepts have already missed the point, their fundamental observation is not entirely wrong. Kumon does not devote textbook pages to the explanation of new ideas. Kumon's worksheets simply present the new idea (let's say subtraction), offer examples and a few sample problems, and then let students work their way through several dozen subtraction problems. In a sense, Kumon skips the lecture about the theory of swimming in favor of a brief, to-the-point explanation and a quick demonstration of what swimming looks like, and then tells kids to dive in. And, as Kumon instructors report time and again, the vast majority of children do very well. What about the few who don't get it right away? The instructor is right there to answer questions in as much detail as that child requires. While the Kumon worksheets do not deal at any length with concepts in the abstract, Kumon instructors give hints when necessary to help make the problems easier to understand.

In practice, the instructor already knows, for example, that Johnnie's worksheets for today include the introduction to subtraction. She is waiting and watching to see how much trouble he has with the new operation. If he has a question, she is right there. After she explains the new operation, she'll ask him to try to solve more problems and she'll watch to see how he does on them. If he has trouble, she may assign the same batch of worksheets over and over again until, gradually, he is able to do the whole set comfortably. When he can breeze through that set, she knows he's got the hang of it. Time to move on to the next batch of worksheets, some of which will present exactly the same kind of problems as before and some of which will challenge him with slightly more difficult problems. The idea is to:

1) keep the student from getting discouraged
2) reinforce the material just learned

3) develop the student's skills just a little bit more
    than at the previous level.

In this way, the worksheets always bring students up
the "Kumon path" slowly, but always with a firm footing.
Maintaining confidence in one's abilities even when faced
with new material is part of the key to developing a successful attitude. This is one of the strongest features of the
Kumon Method.

One big advantage of the Kumon study materials is
that they enable instructors to identify each student's individual weak areas and problems, with pinpoint accuracy.
Personalized help is far more useful for the student when the
exact problem area is known. The Kumon Method virtually
guarantees that any difficulty a child is having with the
worksheets will be discovered by the instructor who will
then address that problem with personalized guidance.

The same is true of the materials themselves. Perhaps
not just one student, but many students may be having
trouble with a certain unit. It may not be the students' lack
of comprehension at all, but rather a series of problems that
are a bit too difficult for them. During my visit to the
Kumon Institute of Education, in Osaka, Japan, I learned
about a special group within the Institute responsible for
revising the thousands of worksheets in the Kumon programs. Unlike textbooks, which are often used unchanged
for many years, the Kumon worksheets are completely re-
evaluated to identify and eliminate specific problem areas
every year. The Institute's team has reports from Kumon
centers all across Japan and around the world to help them

in identifying problems with and developing revisions for specific worksheets. Hypothetically, let's suppose that thousands of Kumon centers report that one particular sub-level of ten worksheets at level B or C is taking many students more than ten re-tries to reach the standard completion time range, while the sets just before and after it require less than five tries. Obviously some of the problems in those sheets are too difficult and may need to be revised. Although almost all the kinks have been ironed out of the system during the past thirty-five years, there are always small points that merit closer attention.

The Kumon Institute team does its work, the new worksheets are printed and distributed to Kumon centers, and then incoming data is monitored closely to see if their revisions are sufficient. If after a year or so of observing data, the results are still not as smooth as they should be, this section can be revised yet again, the data can be monitored again, and the process continued until the revision is completely satisfactory. (This kind of fine-tuning of teaching materials is something that textbook publishers can only dream about.)

5A 61

5A 61a   Exercises with Lines 7

Date: _____, 19_____

Name: _____

Let's draw a line from the dot ● to the star ★

tulip

5A

This set of materials is aimed at improving children's manual dexterity and writing ability. Beginning with practice in drawing short, straight lines, it is designed so that children naturally acquire penmanship skills that allow them to write numbers and letters clearly and easily. Working with these materials also trains the children to concentrate on answering the worksheets.

4A

The children practice writing numbers using the penmanship skills acquired from the 5A level materials. As they count the number of circles or fill in the number charts up to 100, they also acquire a firm grasp of the order in which the numbers are arranged. It is important that they practice reciting numbers at the same time.

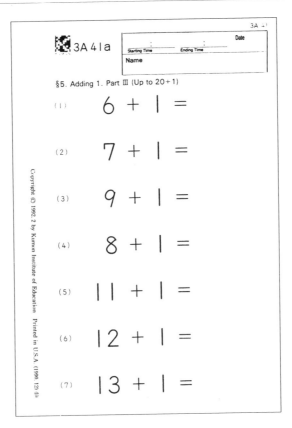

3A

After further practice in arranging numbers in order, the children begin addition. This set of materials covers practice from "1+" through "3+." It has been demonstrated that children who can recite the numbers 1 to 30 find adding +1 easy to solve.

Materials are arranged so that children first practice "+1," and when this has been thoroughly mastered, advance to "+2." Only when they can handle both of these smoothly do they proceed to "+3." In this way, children can make progress easily throughout their study of addition.

2A 13 a

2A 13!

Date

Starting Time   Ending Time

Name

§14. Adding 8. Part II (Up to 15 + 8)

(1) $2 + 8 =$

(2) $1 + 8 =$

(3) $3 + 8 =$

(4) $5 + 8 =$

(5) $6 + 8 =$

(6) $10 + 8 =$

(7) $7 + 8 =$

(8) $8 + 8 =$

(9) $12 + 8 =$

(10) $11 + 8 =$

2A

This set of materials extends the instruction of basic addition begun in the 3A level materials. By gradually increasing the level of addition from that in the 3A level of materials, in these worksheets, the child practices up to "+10."

Since they have already become familiar with the concept of tens and units from the previous Kumon texts, children encounter little or no difficulty in advancing to the addition of two-digit numbers.

A 181a ☆   Time : to :   Date   A 181

Name

§19. Subtraction VI (From numbers up to 17)

(1) $12 - 6 =$

(2) $12 - 9 =$

(3) $13 - 4 =$

(4) $13 - 6 =$

(5) $13 - 5 =$

(6) $13 - 8 =$

(7) $14 - 5 =$

(8) $14 - 7 =$

(9) $14 - 3 =$

(10) $14 - 11 =$

(11) $14 - 1 =$

(12) $14 - 13 =$

A

The first 80 worksheets give learners the ability to mentally calculate problems like 6+17 or 22+9. Following this, subtraction is introduced and the skill level is developed with the goal of mentally solving problems such as 15-9 or 12-8. Thorough practice in addition at the levels from 3A through A enables children to acquire subtraction skills relatively quickly.

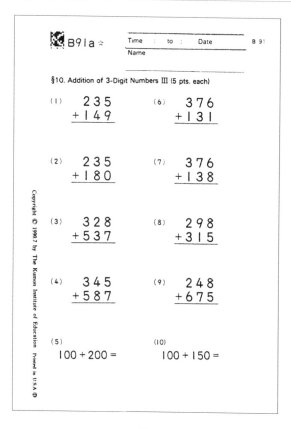

B

Whereas the A level materials present problems written horizontally for mental calculations, the B level materials develop skills in written calculation by working vertically. Both addition and subtraction skills are extended through work with three-digit numbers. As the number of digits increases, the instances of carrying and borrowing also rise, but boxes for the answers are printed on the introductory worksheets so the learners can understand the process naturally by themselves. Word problems are introduced at this level.

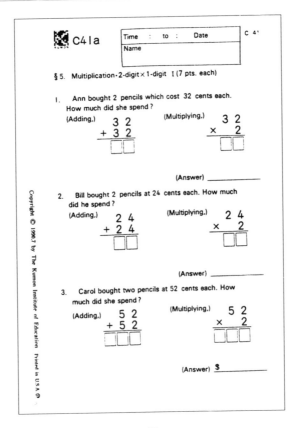

C

Multiplication and division are introduced. Starting with 30 sheets for practicing the tables, exercises in multiplication continue up to one digit times four digits. The division section examines numbers up to three digits divided by one digit. The materials introducing the multiplication tables are especially designed to make them as easy as possible for the child to understand.

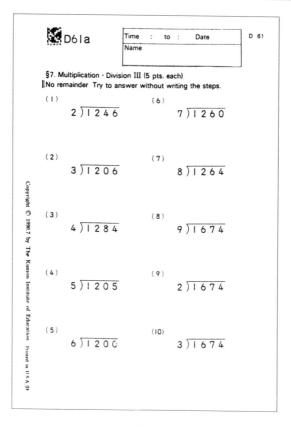

D

Problems involving multipliers and divisors of two or more digits are studied. Particular emphasis is given to division problems with two-digit divisors, focusing on developing the kind of mathematical "sense" that enables the learner to look at the problem and quickly estimate what the quotient will probably be. On the basis of this "sense," the study of fractions is introduced in the last 50 worksheets.

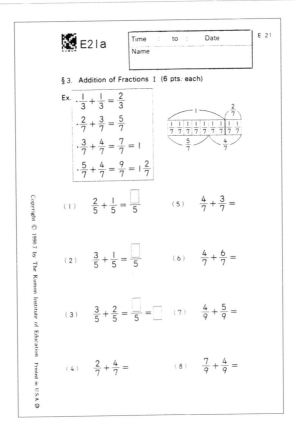

E

The materials give the learner a solid foundation in the four basic operations with fractions. Kumon puts special emphasis on the instruction of calculation with fractions.

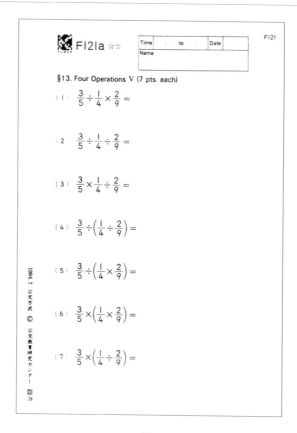

§13. Four Operations V (7 pts. each)

(1) $\dfrac{3}{5} \div \dfrac{1}{4} \times \dfrac{2}{9} =$

(2) $\dfrac{3}{5} \div \dfrac{1}{4} \div \dfrac{2}{9} =$

(3) $\dfrac{3}{5} \times \dfrac{1}{4} \div \dfrac{2}{9} =$

(4) $\dfrac{3}{5} \div \left(\dfrac{1}{4} \div \dfrac{2}{9} \right) =$

(5) $\dfrac{3}{5} \div \left(\dfrac{1}{4} \times \dfrac{2}{9} \right) =$

(6) $\dfrac{3}{5} \times \left(\dfrac{1}{4} \times \dfrac{2}{9} \right) =$

(7) $\dfrac{3}{5} \times \left(\dfrac{1}{4} \div \dfrac{2}{9} \right) =$

F

Mixed operations are performed on fairly complicated fractions. Children who have acquired the skills up through this level find the study of math is made easier.

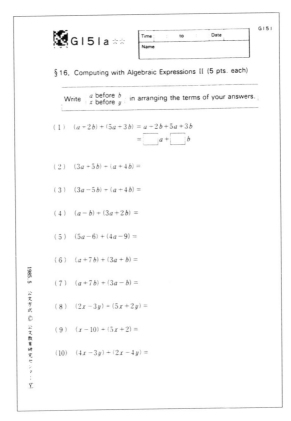

G151a ☆☆

| Time | : | to | : | Date |
| Name | | | | |

G151

§16. Computing with Algebraic Expressions II (5 pts. each)

Write $\dfrac{a \text{ before } b}{x \text{ before } y}$ in arranging the terms of your answers.

(1) $(a + 2b) + (5a + 3b) = a - 2b + 5a + 3b$
$= \boxed{}\,a + \boxed{}\,b$

(2) $(3a + 5b) + (a + 4b) =$

(3) $(3a - 5b) + (a + 4b) =$

(4) $(a - b) + (3a + 2b) =$

(5) $(5a - 6) + (4a - 9) =$

(6) $(a + 7b) + (3a + b) =$

(7) $(a + 7b) + (3a - b) =$

(8) $(2x - 3y) + (5x + 2y) =$

(9) $(x - 10) + (5x + 2) =$

(10) $(4x - 3y) + (2x - 4y) =$

1985. 5 公文方式 Ⓒ 公文教育研究センター ：Ⅴ

G

These materials give the learner mastery of calculation with positive and negative numbers and the fundamentals of algebra, such as calculating expressions containing letters as symbols. Children who have so far known only positive numbers tend to get confused when negative numbers are introduced. Therefore, the first half of this set of materials concentrates on thorough practice in positive and negative numbers. Likewise, as preparation for starting equations in the H level materials, the value of algebraic equations and calculation of expressions is thoroughly practiced.

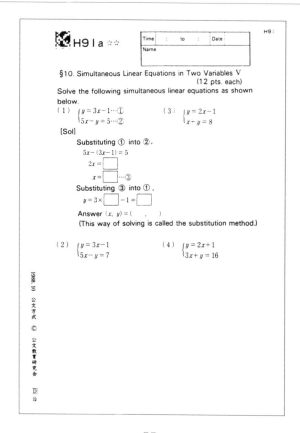

H9 I

§10. Simultaneous Linear Equations in Two Variables V
(12 pts. each)
Solve the following simultaneous linear equations as shown below.

(1) $\begin{cases} y = 3x - 1 \cdots ① \\ 5x - y = 5 \cdots ② \end{cases}$ (3) $\begin{cases} y = 2x - 1 \\ x + y = 8 \end{cases}$

[Sol]

Substituting ① into ②,

$5x - (3x - 1) = 5$

$2x = \boxed{}$

$x = \boxed{} \cdots ③$

Substituting ③ into ①,

$y = 3 \times \boxed{} - 1 = \boxed{}$

Answer $(x, y) = (\quad , \quad)$
(This way of solving is called the substitution method.)

(2) $\begin{cases} y = 3x - 1 \\ 5x - y = 7 \end{cases}$ (4) $\begin{cases} y = 2x + 1 \\ 3x + y = 16 \end{cases}$

1988. 10 公文方式 © 公文教育研究会 D 19

H

The H level materials teach simple equations through simultaneous linear equations with four variables. Solving equations, checking them over, and verifying the numbers often seems to give children a sense of satisfaction—the feeling that they are really doing mathematics.

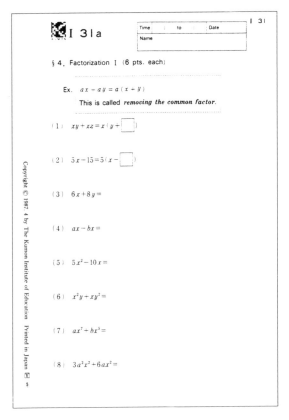

§ 4. Factorization I (6 pts. each)

Ex. $ax - ay = a(x + y)$

This is called *removing the common factor.*

(1) $xy + xz = x(y + \boxed{})$

(2) $5x - 15 = 5(x - \boxed{})$

(3) $6x + 8y =$

(4) $ax - bx =$

(5) $5x^2 - 10x =$

(6) $x^2y + xy^2 =$

(7) $ax^7 + bx^5 =$

(8) $3a^2x^2 + 6ax^2 =$

I

This set of materials gives mastery over factorization, square roots and quadratic equations. The I level materials provide an important bridge to more advanced mathematics. As factoring ability is particularly important for later study, this set of materials contains 60 sheets of factoring problems, arranged in small steps.

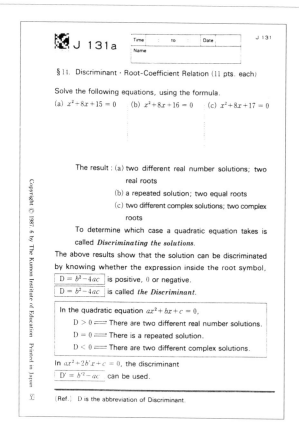

§11. Discriminant · Root-Coefficient Relation (11 pts. each)

Solve the following equations, using the formula.

(a) $x^2 + 8x + 15 = 0$ (b) $x^2 + 8x + 16 = 0$ (c) $x^2 + 8x + 17 = 0$

The result : (a) two different real number solutions; two real roots

(b) a repeated solution; two equal roots

(c) two different complex solutions; two complex roots

To determine which case a quadratic equation takes is called *Discriminating the solutions.*

The above results show that the solution can be discriminated by knowing whether the expression inside the root symbol,

$D = b^2 - 4ac$ is positive, 0 or negative.

$D = b^2 - 4ac$ is called *the Discriminant.*

In the quadratic equation $ax^2 + bx + c = 0$,

$D > 0 \Longrightarrow$ There are two different real number solutions.

$D = 0 \Longrightarrow$ There is a repeated solution.

$D < 0 \Longrightarrow$ There are two different complex solutions.

In $ax^2 + 2b'x + c = 0$, the discriminant

$D' = b'^2 - ac$ can be used.

(Ref.) D is the abbreviation of Discriminant.

J to Q

The materials from levels J through Q cover advanced mathematics. The goal of Kumon is to enable the learner to solve these problems without undue effort. The I level materials are preparation for this. If learners have a complete command of the skills up through I level, they will have little trouble in solving the advanced math level materials which begin with level J.

Chapter 4

Is Kumon Effective?

At first, all of this talk about carefully designed course materials, a comfortable starting point, the emphasis on accuracy and speed, and so on, sounded very reasonable, but not necessarily convincing. The explanations I heard from Kumon instructors made sense to me, but then I am neither a math teacher nor a child psychologist. In the early stages of my research, I found myself wanting to believe that the method works just like they said it does, but also wanting proof of some kind. Ultimately, I found that proof in dozens of testimonials from parents who witnessed their children's improvement. But to begin with, I wanted to see hard facts. and figures.

As the private Kumon centers do not administer to students any standard national exams to determine conclusive "Before and After" results, there is no empirical way to measure the growth of Kumon's students other than by parental observation. However, in places where the Kumon Method is used as part of an in-school math program, the schools have made the effort to take some measurement of student performance, before and after Kumon, in order to justify continuing with the Method as a regular part of their school program. As you might expect, the results are quite similar from one school to the next and support the comments I have heard from parents all throughout North America.

• At the Cleora Public School in Oklahoma, the Kumon Method was introduced in January of 1990 for approximately 130 students. A comparison of Iowa Test of Basic Skills scores from early 1990 to April, 1993 shows a marked improvement in math ability. The average for the entire group, grades 1-8, in total Math (which includes concepts, computation, and problem-solving) rose from the 63rd percentile to the 82nd percentile. Average Math Computation scores alone rose even more: 63% to 84%. Although the smallest school in the county, in 1993, Cleora placed 1st in the 6th and 7th grade divisions of the "Math Counts Contest." Superintendent of Cleora Public School, Woodrow Goins, remarked, "In my 30 years in education it is the most outstanding program we've ever been involved in."

• In Dundee, Illinois, students at St. Catherine of Siena School also took the Iowa Test of Basic Skills twice, once in 1990 and again in 1992. After two years of Kumon study, the increase in test scores was dramatic. In 1990, St. Catherine's 3rd graders scored in the 39th percentile in Computation and 56th percentile in Total Math. Two years later, taking the test in 5th grade, these same students scored 81% in Computation and 77% in Total Math. Their older counterparts nearly matched their success. The 5th grade class posted scores of 56th percentile in Computation and 72% in Total Math in 1990. In 1992, the 7th graders scored in the 74th and 79th percentiles, respectively.

And more....

• In 1990, the Christ Episcopal School in Texas began a trial program, using the Kumon Method in its regular math courses. Two groups of students—second graders and fifth graders—were chosen to determine whether or not Kumon can be effective in raising math scores within a relatively short period of time. Both groups had been tested the year before with a standard Stanford Achievement Test. Although less than a year had passed since introducing the Kumon system, the school authorities were interested to see if it had produced any measurable effects. The results speak for themselves.

Stanford Achievement Test Results

2nd Grade	1989	1990
Overall Math	53	81
Concepts	58	89
Application	49	76
Computation	49	76
5th Grade		
Overall Math	76	94
Concepts	76	92
Application	70	85
Computation	71	94

• In Bowie, Maryland, after three years of static test scores (1988-1990), students at Holy Trinity Episcopal Day

School have seen their scores on the MAT 6 (Massachu-setts Achievement Test) jump. At Holy Trinity, 210 students, in grades 1-6 took Kumon for five months in 1991 and for the entire year in 1992. These students' average Problem-Solving score rose from 80% in 1990 to 86% in 1992. In Computa-tion, their scores increased from 72% in 1990, before Kumon, to 88% in 1992.

• Another striking example comes from Sanford, Colorado, where the Kumon Method was used with students in grades 3-6, but not in 1-2. After only one year of Kumon, the results were impressive. On their april, 1991 Iowa Test of Basic Skills, the 1st Graders showed an average 1% decline, and the 2nd Grades an average of -2%. Of the classes studying Kumon, however, the lowest <u>increase</u> was 9%, while two grades showed a +10% improvement each and one grade averaged +11% increase in performance.

My kids' concentration levels and attention spans have increased noticeably. They can stick with one activity for much longer than they used to. I've seen a big difference in their math grades, and both of them have gone up a full grade in school as a result.

–Sara Rathé, mother, Illinois

Six months before we started with the Kumon program, my son Randy took some California Achievement Tests. His math score was in the 12th percentile. I was horrified. I worked with him over the summer, doing math flash cards and other things, but I knew it just wasn't reaching him. A few months later we started Kumon and everything changed. You could see it in the way he worked at home. Less than a year after he started, he took the same Achievement Tests again. He scored in the 87th percentile. I feel the improvement was directly attributable to Kumon.

–Jane Condry, mother, San Francisco

I used to get Bs and Cs in school, now I'm getting all As and Bs. Kumon's really helped my study habits; it's a lot easier to concentrate now...It's hard to explain, but you do real good in math and you want to keep going, do well in language and geography and other stuff. It feels real good when you get good grades, so you want to keep doing it. I'm really proud because I'm doing great in school. You don't want to let yourself down.

–Matthew Klein, 12, New York

Kumon improves your study habits. It's fun, I want to keep going, I want to do it all, go all the way through the program. You know it helps you so you want to do more. It gives you a lot of pride. I like that.

–Alicia Moseby, 10, Washington

Travis was having trouble with his school math. His Iowa test scores had dropped from the 90th percentile to the 60th, and I was worried. I talked to the school administrators and decided I had to do something. That's when we started Kumon. Now his Iowa math tests are all in the 96th and 99th percentile. But it's not only the math where I see improvement. His spelling and punctuation shot up, too. Kumon has had a big impact all around.

–Ralph Will, father, Virginia

Chapter 5

Is Kumon Right For My Child?

Many parents I spoke with who had heard or read about the Kumon Method wondered if it would be ideal for other children, but not for theirs. Some parents worry that their children are not yet old enough to begin studying with Kumon. Others worry about children with physical handicaps or learning disabilities. Some of what I discovered in my travels provides answers to these questions.

Are pre-school children too young for Kumon?

From what I have learned, this is the easiest question to answer: No, absolutely, positively not. Pre-school children are ideal learners, and Kumon is one of the best ways to introduce them to the joys of learning. Many a parent asks if their five year-old son or daughter should wait a year or perhaps two before starting the program. Many a Kumon instructor, it turns out, has had to resist the temptation to say, "Why have you waited this long?" The answer is that four-year-olds, even three-year-olds, can benefit tremendously from an early start in Kumon.

We're very happy. It's been really beneficial for both of my kids. We started our daughter about four months after our son joined because we could see the value of starting early.
                              —Mary Freedman, mother, Chicago

I suspect that if Toru Kumon could recreate the world he would insure that every child on the planet began some kind of structured education from about the age of six months. Remember that the Kumon philosophy centers not on math, but on the child, on the potential of every child to develop further and faster than adults ever expect. A child's mind is a flower waiting to bloom. Unlike the child's body, which will take a decade and a half to grow to 80% of its adult size, their brains will be close to full size within a very few years. Yet because the body is small and fragile, we assume the mind is likewise. The result is that we try to "protect" their minds from too much information. Years of research show that this is a monumental fallacy.

While no one would recommend sitting a two-year-old down and forcing him or her to study for five hours a day, it is a fact that even very young children can acquire enormous amounts of information with no apparent effort. The real problem is not their ability, which is almost limitless, but their attention span. For this reason, formal education must be limited to short doses, fifteen minutes here and fif-

Although pre-school children have relatively short attention spans, their potential to learn has been proven to be almost limit-less. Kumon's thirty-five years of experience shows that most parents are not in danger of starting their children in a learning program too early, but are more likely to start them too late.

teen minutes there. Once children discover the pleasure of drawing and learning figures (together with friends of the same age and a caring instructor), there is almost no limit to their potential to grow.

This is not simply some abstract theory proposed by academic psychologists, but the findings of thirty-five years of Kumon instruction. In the early years, even Toru Kumon did not realize the potential of the young mind. It is only through time and the results of so many children studying in Kumon centers around the world that the reality has become apparent. For example, it took nineteen years from the founding of the Kumon Institute of Education before a pre-school student was able to solve equations. Equations are introduced in the Japanese system in the 7th grade, and in the United States and Canada usually a bit later. For an elementary school child to be able to handle equations easily is quite a feat, but for a pre-school child to do so seems amazing. At least it did in 1977 when two young children advanced in their individual Kumon studies to the point where they were working with equations. Even then, the youngest of the two was six years old. By 1988, the youngest student working with equations was twenty-six months old (a record that still stands). In 1992 alone, over 600 pre-school children reached this level. In a few years the figure will probably be several times that many.

Needless to say, these children are bright. Before they enter first grade they are able to solve equations with three or even four variables. Will these children ever fear a math test in their lives? Not likely. Will they be considered freaks or child prodigies? Not from what I have seen. Nor are they likely to be considered geniuses. They will be thought of as perfectly normal children who simply started Kumon early and got caught up in the joy of learning at their own pace and progressing through the different levels. One survey showed that all pre-schoolers who learn to do equations also develop a very high reading ability.

Kumon is confident that at least 90% of the children who begin their studies at the pre-school age will become outstanding all-around students.

In Japan, many pre-schoolers study reading via the Kumon Method (and learning to read Japanese characters is a much more daunting proposition than learning to read the English alphabet.) Despite the intricacy of the Japanese language, there are students who learn to read the basic characters by the age of two. Currently, The Kumon Institute expects a two-year-old child to learn to read in roughly six months of simple daily study. Parents of two-and three-year-olds say their children read for entertainment rather than watching TV. Aside from putting a lot of baby-sitters out of work, what this means is that the child's intelligence and curiosity will be stimulated by books, their vocabulary will increase dramatically, as will spelling ability, comprehension, and so on.

Does all this sound a bit odd? It shouldn't. Most children are perfectly capable of reading and doing junior high or even high school level math before the age of five. All without "pushing" by parents. By studying a little bit every day—with carefully designed materials such as Kumon provides—any child can achieve remarkable results. A number of Kumon instructors fervently expressed the hope that, in the near future, these results will not be remarkable. They will be taken for granted.

As one instructor said to me, "They are just like flowers. You give them water and watch them blossom. They never fail to amaze you."

There are dozens of useful tools for teaching toddlers these days—music, jigsaw puzzles, tracing games, alphabet cards, and so on. For example, jigsaw puzzles are especially useful because they develop both manual dexterity and the ability to concentrate. Understanding the value of puzzles in learning, Kumon created its own series of jigsaw puzzles, a stepped progression of twenty-four levels of all kinds of puzzles, designed to take the child from very simple (2-piece) constructions to very complex (330-piece) patterns. The puzzles are so popular with young Japanese Kumon students that they have been made commercially available in Japan and sell very well. My own child, Ken, was playing with Kumon puzzles (a present from his grandma) long before I knew anything about Kumon. He loves them. He started off with the simplest ones, learned to do them correctly, and then when he could do them quickly he let Mom and Dad know that he didn't find them very challenging any more and wanted new ones. So we gave him the next puzzle in the progression. He mastered that, then we gave him the next, and after almost two years he still enjoys them. In the process he's learned that both accuracy and speed are sure signs that he has mastered one and is ready for the next.

Based on information obtained from its international network of instructors, Kumon is still developing new materials to stimulate very young minds. More and more parents are realizing that there is no reason to hold their children back. That small, fragile body holds an active, inquisitive mind. It will absorb almost anything presented to it, including mathematics and languages. If your children are old enough to hold a pencil, they are old enough to start Kumon.

Learning-impaired children

Handicapped children often have a number of functions that are completely normal, which means many of them can study in much the same way as other students do. And in some cases, even in the area in which they are considered to be impaired, there is potential for improvement.

Kumon purports that appropriate use of their study materials in a patient, supportive manner will usually lead to an improvement in students' academic ability and often in other forms of development as well. For example, many learning-impaired children have inordinately short attention spans. Yet at Kumon's centers, instructors report that the attention spans of many of these children have increased from a few minutes to nearly an hour. Parents of many of these same children report that, as a side-benefit of the Kumon program, their children have learned to dress themselves, and that motor skills, activity levels, and even appetites have improved.

Needless to say, none of these results are claimed or guaranteed by Kumon, nor in even the best cases would any parent say they happened overnight. Educational progress with almost any child requires time and patience on the part of the parent, and with an impaired child it requires much more. However, if parents truly believe in their child's potential just as Kumon does, this will inevitably be communicated to their child. If the parents of learning-impaired children are supportive, and the study materials are used properly, their children will often discover that they can study, learn, and progress beyond anyone's expectations. Little by little, as the results become apparent, these children also usually discover a greater sense of self-esteem. This alone can lead to more satisfactory performance in other areas as well.

The bottom line is that Kumon can be one useful tool in working with learning-impaired children. However, like any system, it requires time and special attention from both the parents and the instructor.

Dyslexia

While researching Kumon in the New York area, I met several outstanding children. One of them was Danny, a bright, talkative child whose instructor told me that he was one of the most accomplished students in her group. I interviewed Danny and liked him very much. He seemed to me just another of those Kumon kids who are destined to be among the top students in their school. After the interview was over and Danny went into the next room to study, his instructor mentioned that he wasn't always like that, and in fact, his progress had been quite impressive. His mother told me the following story:

"Our son Danny is dyslexic. We took him to see a number of specialists and all of them told us essentially the same thing. He would most likely never be able to function quite the way 'normal' kids do, that his reading and writing would always be affected, and so on. My husband and I tried several specialists, we put him in three different schools, and frankly we began to think that maybe the doctors were right. Then I heard from the mother of one of his friends about Kumon. Danny's math scores were pretty bad, so we thought we'd give it a try. He started with the very lowest levels where they make you draw numbers again and again. At first he drew all his numbers backwards, just as he always had. But as he repeated the homework he began to change. Little by little his motor control improved. First he started drawing his numbers correctly, and then as he continued to practice, they became perfect. I mean absolutely perfect, they look like they'd been printed. We were delighted. Then his math scores started to go up, then his concentration went up, and that pulled up his other grades as well…I don't know what to say.

We spent over $35,000 trying various kinds of special help for Danny and nothing worked. Now we've been doing Kumon for a couple of years, which costs almost nothing in comparison, and we think it's the best thing we've found." All the credit doesn't go to Kumon, of course. Danny's parents and his Kumon instructor supported his efforts unfailingly. But once again a young child proved medical "experts" wrong and demonstrated what Toru Kumon has said for years: none of us knows the true potential of a child in the formative years. As long as we encourage each child to keep trying, there is no clear limit to what he or she can learn.

Other disabilities

In Japan there is a fifth grade Kumon student who is easily solving quadratic equations, finding square roots, and similar higher math functions. The child was autistic. Another child with a severe learning disability is solving simultaneous linear equations and reading at a high school level. She's in the second grade. A ninth grade girl with Down's syndrome began the Kumon program at the age of six; today she's also doing high school-level math. A center for mentally-handicapped children, which introduced the Kumon Method some time ago, reports that, after children began learning Kumon they became more energetic, more willing to do their school homework, ate more, and showed better growth patterns. One of the center's staff members, whose own child was studying three levels beyond her school grade level, said she wondered why Kumon hadn't told her earlier about the merits of the program for handicapped kids.

I asked why Kumon does not advertise or promote these results. The response I received was logical and has to do with the sensitive nature of the problems involved. As medical science does not fully understand these situations, what is beneficial in one child's case may prove of no value in another. Consequently, Kumon makes no therapeutic assertions or promises. The Kumon Method was not developed as a special education technique for learning-disabled or handicapped children, nor does it claim to be a cure for any condition. Yet it is an undeniable fact that parents of children with learning problems and handicaps continue to report that Kumon has helped their children.

Tests at school are no problem. I feel really strong and confident. While everybody else is getting all crazy and worrying about it, I just sit down and do it. On math tests, I usually finish pretty early. After I started Kumon I got in the habit of going back to proofread everything. So even when I took a spelling test, I just went through it all, then went back to look for stupid mistakes. Usually there's some little thing I missed, but now that I check everything I usually get A's. I don't expect to get 100 every time, but I usually do real well. Once the teacher told us not to answer some problems because they were too advanced for us, but I did those problems anyway by mistake. I got 'em all right, of course.

—Martin C., Florida,
a child formerly diagnosed
with a learning disability

Every year Kumon holds a Learning-Impaired Children's Seminar in Japan for students who are physically-handicapped or learning-impaired and their parents. At this seminar, new case studies as well as new approaches are discussed. Over the years, many of these Japanese families have come to Kumon centers for help, almost always through word-of-mouth recommendations.

One of the most famous stories that I encountered in Japan is about a little girl, named Chiemi. Born with Down's syndrome, Chiemi was physically weak, drooled constantly, and was unable to articulate words. Her Kumon instructor saw Chiemi as both a personal and professional challenge and worked with her as if Chiemi were her own daughter.

After more than two years of constant efforts by Chiemi, her parents, and her Kumon instructor, it came time to enroll her in regular school. Chiemi's mother had to stand before a special committee that decides whether a child with Down's syndrome must be placed in a special school for the handicapped. Her mother presented Chiemi's completed Kumon worksheets to the committee who voted to admit Chiemi to a regular school. Gradually her work level picked up, and by fifth grade she was solving quadratic equations.

Chapter 6

Other Questions Parents Often Ask

A
s I traveled around North America, I often heard questions from parents who either had children already studying in Kumon or who were contemplating enrolling their children. Instructors told me the same questions crop up again and again, both from current and prospective Kumon parents. We don't have enough room to discuss them all here, but there are a few that I heard often enough that they deserve to be answered in print for the thousands of parents who may want to ask the same question tomorrow. For example,

Why doesn't Kumon teach concepts?

As I stated earlier, it is a mistake to think that Kumon doesn't teach concepts at all, although it is true that the worksheets concentrate almost exclusively on calculation problems. Concepts are introduced in the materials, but in simple, easy steps, each followed by many problems to reinforce the idea they illustrate. Fundamentally, Kumon believes that young children can both acquire abstract concepts and perform practical tasks such as calculation, but that they are faster and more confident with the latter. That is to say, you can build a rock-solid foundation of addition more successfully by having a child complete hundreds of different kinds of addition problems than by asking that child to read several pages discussing the concept of two apples plus three apples equals five apples.

I regret that the schools have decided to give up emphasizing the basics and gone into this all-conceptual thing with very little drill. I think the kids really understand the concepts better when they already know what's going on. You see it in their faces. All of a sudden the lights come on, and they say "Oh, sure, I know that."

—George Prezioso, father, Chicago

Once children know addition without any question, and can perform it in their heads almost instantly, introducing real-world applications for these same arithmetic operations is fairly simple. However, in the Kumon philosophy, trying to explain concepts to children who cannot yet calculate using addition or who do so imperfectly, is problematic at best. Thus, Kumon drills the "mechanics" of math and introduces the concepts a little at a time.

Kumon instructors point out that when students study new material in math, and you begin by teaching them concepts, there are always parts that they do not understand. This makes it difficult both to do the subsequent practice problems and to understand the concept as a whole.

On the other hand, if you introduce the same concept to students who have already studied up to the level where they are working comfortably with those practice problems, acquiring the new concept that applies to those problems becomes much easier. In other words, Kumon wasn't designed to make teaching easier; it was designed to make learning easier for the student. Like so many other aspects of the Kumon Method, this approach to new concepts has been shown to be successful over and over again through years of experience with very large numbers of students.

There is another point that Kumon instructors say is often overlooked. Some parents—and even some educators —approach Kumon as if it were a substitute for school. This is definitely not the case. In those schools where Kumon is used regularly, it usually serves as an adjunct to their normal math programs.

One day Timmy was sick and brought home his math book. He was supposed to divide a 2-digit number and I knew that he didn't know his multiplication tables. I was curious about how he was going to do division without knowing multiplication. That led me to ask the school officials what they were teaching, and they said it was a conceptual, hands-on manipulative approach to math. I said, "Hey, that's great, but what about his arithmetic? He can't even add and subtract and you're asking him to multiply and divide," and they said, "That will come. We don't reach for mas-

*tery at this age level, but it will come." I didn't buy into that.
Then I discovered that once kids can handle simple arithmetic—
whenever that 'comes'—the school wants them to use a calculator for everything. I knew it was time to look for something else.
There had to be a better way. For us, Kumon is it… I will also
say that Kumon alone is not enough. I think kids need the
emphasis on conceptualization as well, but the two go hand in
hand. Kumon plus regular school is a terrific combination.*

—Jane Rowlands, mother, San Francisco

In private centers, Kumon is an after-school activity, not a replacement for school. In the child's regular school math class the teacher explains the conceptual framework of mathematics first and establishes drill and practice time second. Kumon recognizes, however, that it is impossible for even a very dedicated teacher working with exceptionally cooperative students to find time for both detailed conceptual work and rigorous practice. Thus, the Kumon Method supplies the child with the drills and practice necessary to guarantee that concepts are not merely "learned today and forgotten tomorrow."

It is interesting to note, however, that a very large number of Kumon students report that they get ahead of their normal grade level in school and then, when concepts are introduced in their math classes the children already understand them. If Kumon were not helping kids to understand math concepts, both through explanation and through practice leading to conceptual understanding, children would always be encountering entirely new ideas in regular school. Instead, they always say school seems more like "review" than first-time learning.

Matt Lupsha, Kumon General Manager in Cincinnati, Ohio summed it for me quite well when he related the following analogy:

When children are learning the piano, you don't teach them composition first. You learn scales first, and you drill them again and again, and then you practice simple songs, and then you move up slowly to more and more difficult practice pieces. At each step you repeat work constantly, drilling it so that the lessons contained in each piece stay with the student for life. In the same way, you then introduce music theory, composition and so on in a gradual way, and only when you are sure the student has a firm foundation in the basics. So it is with Kumon.

Isn't Kumon really just for Asian kids?

This is not as foolish a question as you might think. Quite a number of parents wonder about the background of the program and its suitability for students from western cultures. Of course Kumon was developed in Japan, but it has long since spread around the world, and is growing especially rapidly across the United States and Canada. The worksheets have all been carefully translated and a large number of the instructors are non-Asian. So why are there so many Japanese, Chinese, Korean, and Indian students? A look at the Kumon "honor roll" for North America always shows a large number of Asian names. What's going on?

Kumon's beginnings were in Japan, but it soon spread around the world. Kumon is a completely democratic method, through which all children can develop their untapped potential regardless of race, creed, color, or social background.

The answer is very simple, and it has nothing to do with where the Kumon Method originated. The fact is that most Asian families place enormous importance on education. Throughout history these societies have emphasized learning. Children who could not read and write as well as quote from classical literature at an early age were considered uneducated. Their parents have stressed study to a degree uncommon in most European and North American homes. In Japan, for example, where children already attend public school an average of sixty more days per year than in the United States, it is very common for parents to send their children to after-school *juku* (special tutoring schools) where they study the same subjects, only more intensively.

Add to this the fact that most Asian families in North America are first- or second-generation citizens. They want their children to have every advantage for getting ahead in this society, and excelling academically is the surest way to acceptance at a top graduate or professional school and to land a high-paying job. Thus, it is only natural for Asian-American parents to look for an academic "edge" that will help their children succeed in this extremely competitive western society.

As a result, in some parts of the country there are many Asian students enrolled in Kumon centers. As one non-Asian parent in Connecticut said to me, "A few months after I heard about the first Kumon center opening in our area I discovered that all the Japanese kids and most of the Chinese kids in our town were enrolling. That's how I knew it must be good. Those parents are very serious when it comes to education. I put both my kids in as well—that was about a year ago—and now my daughter is the top math student in her grade."

The ironic thing is that this same academic edge is available to everyone. Any child can go to Kumon and any child can excel. All the worksheets and other materials are in English, and so is the instruction. We are all concerned about the education of our children, and we should all be looking for any practical method that will help them to develop their natural talents. Kumon is certainly a time-tested approach that can work for just about anyone.

Is all that repetition really necessary?

This is one of the biggest problems parents seem to have with the Kumon Method, though it doesn't seem to bother their children much at all. As we have seen, Kumon emphasizes repetition. Children have to solve the same kind of problem again and again on a single worksheet, then complete several more worksheets that are only slightly different. After that, they face very similar problems in the worksheets at the next set, and then complete even more of the same problems in the achievement test at the end of that level. This is not poor planning on the part of the Kumon worksheet designers—just the reverse. Decades of Kumon research have shown that there is nothing more helpful to students for really learning their math basics than constant repetition.

Consider for example, one of the early worksheets in

Instructors such as Ann Hui of Toronto know that every child can achieve through Kumon. Her center in Toronto has more than 1,200 students and is still growing.

the addition section. A child begins addition with problems involving adding 1 to another number. The first several worksheets will ask the student to add 1 (and always 1) to a long column of numbers. Of course, the child quickly masters that and goes on to the next step: adding 2 (and always 2) to a series of numbers. Accuracy is easy to achieve, and gradually the student understands this process of simple addition well enough that speed comes by itself. The child is ready to move on. To an adult, this seems incredibly boring. Constant repetition of very simple exercises seems a sure way to kill anyone's interest in any subject. To children, however, it is just the opposite. How many times have we seen our children spend hours playing with something that we tired of watching in the first few minutes? The "tedious" aspects of Kumon are much more the perception of adults watching the work than they are of the children doing the work.

Moreover, children delight in solving so many problems and especially in solving them all correctly. They are achieving visible mastery over something highly abstract, and both the instructor and Mom and Dad are full of praise. Who could be bored?

For just this reason, the teacher who tries to "help" very young students by jumping quickly from one step to another is doing them a great disservice. Trying to force children to move quickly from adding one to adding five and then to adding ten is like asking a young toddler to walk only a few steps and then to run. There may be a few children in a thousand who can do it, but the vast majority will stumble along, trying to please their teacher and afraid to say that they really do not understand. It is precisely this situation that the Kumon Method is trying to counter.

Parents and instructors alike sometimes fall into the trap of trying to "move the system along," by which they really mean move the child through some of the material at a faster pace. Although the child may be scoring in the 90s on worksheets, there may still be some unanswered questions or some careless mistakes. The way to eliminate that once and for all is to repeat a set of ten worksheets. Some parents impatiently try to pressure their child's instructor not to "hold the child back," and, sad to say, some new instructors give in to this pressure and reluctantly do not require a child to redo a unit. Rather than helping the child to advance, this has just the opposite effect. If a student simply tries to progress through the levels quickly, not redoing worksheets and even ignoring the SCTs so as to reach a higher level sooner, it is almost guaranteed that this student will reach a point where progress hits a wall. On the other hand, the child who works diligently and repeats work as often as needed, will rise through the levels smoothly.

While there are officially 200 worksheets at each level, it is assumed that many will be repeated, and some repeated several times. Unfortunately, there are some students who complete only about 240 or 250 worksheets in a level when they should probably be doing twice that many. The end result is often a child who "sort of " understands, but hasn't really mastered mathematical operations.

To put this in perspective, let's look at Kumon in

Why are we so worried about repetition in school? Every job I can think of requires at least some repetitive work, and we accept that. We understand how vital repetition is in learning to play a sport or a musical instrument, but we still don't see how similar the situation is for math. We should be saying to our children, "Sure math is hard, but if you keep practicing you can do it. Math is like learning the piano or learning to hit a fastball. You practice and practice, and then you'll discover you can do it easily." But instead we say, "You already understand the concepts, and I know you can do the problems. You must be bored by having to repeat this work." We are thus unwittingly providing the perfect excuse for future failure.

In math, the need for overlearning is the justification for repetition. Unlike other subjects, math skills must be overlearned at each stage in order for the student to be successful in later stages.

—Dr. Patricia L. Hollingsworth,
Director, University of Tulsa
School for Gifted Children

Japan, where there is already plenty of data on how often students repeat work. I was surprised to discover that many Kumon instructors in Japan recommend that students repeat all or most of a level a few times.

Some of the very best students complete several hundred worksheets for each level. Of course the amount of repetition necessary to master an operation varies from individual to individual, but the Kumon people say they know that repetition helps to solidify understanding and so is unquestionably a good thing. It helps the student. It should never be looked at as punishment; repeating worksheets is a completely normal part of the program. There are cases where top-notch students may do a total of a thousand worksheets at some level. "Practice makes perfect" may sound like a shopworn homily, but, from what I have seen, no greater proof exists of its importance for children in learning math than its effectiveness in Kumon.

Kumon's records (for Japan) indicate that almost every child who has studied with the Kumon Method in the past thirty-five years has had to go back and re-do many worksheets. The Kumon philosophy accepts that this is an important part of the learning process. Repetition fosters improved understanding, which inevitably results in improved performance.

Why is speed so important?

Many parents are understandably concerned with Kumon's emphasis on Standard Completion Times (SCT.) Especially in teaching elementary school students. For example, it is natural to question how Kumon can reconcile its belief that education must be interesting and help to motivate the child with its insistence that students meet certain time guidelines.

"Are you trying to prepare young children for time tests in high school?" is a familiar question. "Are you trying to turn our children into robots who perform according to a stop watch?" is less often voiced, but probably just as common a fear. The answer to both questions is no.

Kumon is not trying to turn students into speed demons. The idea of speed itself as a goal has no meaning. The purpose of the SCT is simply to demonstrate the student's mastery of one step of the learning process, which is a clear sign of being prepared to begin the next step. For example, consider a normal case of a child who cannot complete a series of worksheets accurately. Is that child ready to move on to more difficult work? Of course not. In the same way, Kumon considers the child who can obtain the correct answers, but only after an unusually long time thinking about it, as not yet ready to move on. This is perfectly normal. Do not get the impression that there is some select group of kids who zip through all the worksheets quickly, while the "slower" kids can't get over the SCT hurdle. This is not the case. Almost every child working through the Kumon system first learns to solve new problems using material just introduced, and then by a process of repetition internalizes this process. That is, children go over the material again and again until the knowledge is fully

Knowing the correct answer is not enough. Reaching it relatively quickly demonstrates a student's level of understanding of a specific concept.

absorbed. In the process of doing so, each child naturally becomes faster at doing this kind of problem. When a child has completely mastered the work, achieving the SCT targets comes naturally.

The principle underlying this is really quite simple, and talking about standard completion times sometimes makes it seem more complicated than it needs to be. Let's look at a simple example. Suppose your daughter is working with addition. Her worksheets require her to add 8 + 2, 9 + 2, and so on. She can figure out the answers eventually by counting on her fingers. That's good. It means she understands the concept of addition. But just arriving at the right answer doesn't mean she has "learned" addition in a way that will be useful to her in the future. As she goes on to do more complicated math in school or even in a real world situation, she will not have time to count on her fingers; she won't even have time to use a calculator. To master addition means to be able to produce sums in your head instantaneously. When you say to her "8 + 2" and she answers back immediately "10!," you know that she has learned to calculate using addition. You are probably not aware that you are mentally timing her, but let's just imagine that she took half a minute to give you the answer. Then you would know instinctively that something was wrong. Of course you don't have a set time in mind—she doesn't have to give you the answer in one or two seconds. We assume it takes time for a young child to be able to verbalize an answer. But if she takes more than a reasonable amount of time, say, more than five seconds in this case, it means she still needs more drill in basic addition problems.

In essence, the standard completion times are very much like this example. That is, the SCT for any worksheet is not a specific target time, not some arbitrary goal that your child must meet. Instead, it is a target time range which has been shown to be a realistic goal for millions of students. In other words, Kumon's program does not specify: "This worksheet must be completed in one and a half minutes." Rather, the SCT range indicates that any student the world over, who really understands the material at that level, should be able to finish the worksheet in somewhere between two and four minutes. Many will finish closer to two minutes and some closer to four. Any student who takes between five and six minutes to complete the same work is not yet really comfortable with the material. Substantial research has shown that these completion ranges are reasonable and that almost all children who have mastered the materials will attain them with ease.

Once again, this does not mean that your child will start a new set of worksheets and immediately finish in the target time range. The first time around almost every child has difficulty with some of the problems. This is normal. They repeat work. This, too, is normal. Two or three weeks later the same child will be able to complete the same worksheets quickly and accurately. That child is ready for something a little bit more challenging. This is one of the basic principles of the Kumon Method.

Does learning to concentrate their abilities so as to work quickly and accurately really help children to prepare for tests later on in school? Of course it does. Does it help them to feel more confident about test-taking at all levels?

Yes, of course it does. But Kumon views these as side benefits, not the original intention behind the development of
ideal completion time ranges.

I think he's much more conscious of the time it takes to do his
work now. He allows enough time to go back and check things
when he's done... I think there's a lot less intimidation in being
presented with a stack of work and a set time to do it in, whether
it's a test or just an assignment or whatever, because they're pre-
sented with that on a daily basis in Kumon. Things that seem to
be overwhelming for other kids are less so for people who have
spent time in Kumon.

—Jaye Smith, mother, Pennsylvania

What do I need to do as a Kumon parent?

So many parents these days are busy, it seems harder than
ever for them to devote as much time as they would like to
their child's education. One of the advantages of public
schools in many parts of the country is that you simply
make sure your children are awake and dressed in the morning, see them off to the school bus, and turn your mind to
other things until the bus brings them home again in the
afternoon. This, I can assure you, is not Kumon.

Parents who decide to enroll their children in Kumon
realize that education requires a mutual commitment. Each
child must learn to work alone, to concentrate on home-

When I started my 3rd grade math class, I brought along some of the simultaneous linear equations I was doing at the time in Kumon and worked some of those out for my teacher. He was real impressed. One of the other math teachers in the school has his own kids in Kumon.

—Amanda Gann, 7, Maine.

Every now and then I tell Amanda that she can drop out any time, but she doesn't want to. I think she's a lot more confident about a lot of things as a result of Kumon. She feels she can master just about anything that's thrown at her.

—Amanda's Dad

work, and to do it every day. Each parent must make a commitment as well. The biggest commitment comes in the first couple of months when parents must see that homework is done daily. Kumon keeps the assignments short so that the burden is small, but doing them all on Sunday night defeats the purpose of the program. Children need to develop good study habits and learn self-discipline. To help children accomplish this, either Mom or Dad (or preferably both) must enforce strict rules, especially the rule that calls for about twenty minutes of every day for Kumon homework. No excuses, no exceptions.

At the same time, parents must support their children emotionally. This is easier because it is something we naturally want to do, but all too often we forget to give our support regularly. Kumon asks parents to show children how pleased they are with their children's performance. When their children start doing their homework every day, Kumon calls for a little "positive reinforcement." When they start to advance from one unit to the next and then from one level to the next, children want praise from the people they respect most. When the problems become difficult and children find they have to work much harder just to complete a few nights' homework, Kumon knows that encouragement from Mom and Dad can be a big help. A few sincere words is all it takes, but this, too, is part of your commitment as a Kumon parent.

In some centers in North America, parents also correct homework. An answer book is provided so this is simple to do and takes little time. It is also something many parents come to enjoy. As one parent told me, "When your son or daughter is in school, you have no idea what they're learning or how well they're learning it. They may be staring out the window all day for all you know. And sometimes kids who don't do very well are given passing grades anyway, so even their report cards don't mean what they used to. If you have a child in Kumon, you know every day, every week of the year exactly what he or she is studying and how well that child is doing. After just a few weeks you'll come to really appreciate that. You'll see your child come up against new, unfamiliar material, struggle with it for a while, and then burst through and do it like it was second nature. You'll watch your child repeat a unit and repeat and repeat and then all of a sudden, Bang! He's got it, and he's passing an achievement test and starting a new level. It's a wonderful feeling, and one you don't get anywhere else."

Last, there is the relatively minor, but still troublesome commitment of time during a busy day. Children need to go to a Kumon center twice a week for about thirty minutes each time. In many cases, someone has to take them there, and usually sit and wait for them to finish. Again, for many people this may seem like an extremely small time commitment each week, but for working parents it is not easy. And yet, many people find ways to manage it. In fact, many Kumon parents told me they enjoyed talking with both the other parents at the center and with the instructors. Perhaps more importantly, many parents find that one of the biggest side benefits for them is the "hands on" contact with their child's education.

Nicholas does Kumon every day. And that means every day, Saturdays, Sundays, holidays, his birthday, every day. He usually works for 15-20 minutes first thing in the morning. I think his frustration level is the lowest in the morning when he's not carrying the baggage of the day. Nowadays he never complains, he just does it.

—Janice McCudden, mother, Ohio

There are days when he likes doing his homework more than others, but he does it every day. Even when we go away on vacation we take our Kumon with us.

—Louise Gifford, mother, New York

The only hard part of Kumon is that first couple of weeks when the child has to get used to doing it every day, but once they get started they get used to it pretty quickly. After that, they tell you, "Mom, I can't go to bed yet. I haven't done my Kumon."

—Yukiko Hayakawa, mother, Boston

Kumon teaches children they have to plan their time, which is good. But it doesn't take a lot of time, which is also good.

—Maryann Bunting, mother, Oklahoma

Are there other benefits to children in Kumon besides learning math?

I think I could probably fill another book just with the comments I heard from parents about what they—and their children—have found in Kumon that they never really expected. Almost without exception, parents who had experienced Kumon for over a year praised the changes they saw in their children's ability to study, to concentrate, and to be responsible for themselves. One of the side benefits of encouraging students to challenge themselves with the standard completion times on both tests and homework is that it forces them to concentrate. Talking, doodling, getting up and running around the room—all of these seem to disappear gradually as the children settle in to the worksheets. They learn to focus their attention squarely on the material at hand, even if only for fifteen minutes at first, and this seems to build a foundation for greater concentration in other endeavors.

In the words of one child's mother, "Just last year my daughter couldn't sit still for five minutes. Getting her to do her Kumon homework at first was pretty tough, but once we got over the first few weeks, she has become almost another person. She's still as wild as ever when she's playing with her friends, but when it comes time to do her Kumon she sits down and works all the way through it. About six months after she started the program one of her teachers—not her math teacher, by the way—told us she'd seen a change in our little girl, how much more attentive she was in class and how she seems a little more interested in what she's learning than before. We weren't surprised. It's obvious that she's learning to focus her attention and that's helping her in school." I heard so many versions of this story that I thought Kumon must be handing out scripts to parents across the country.

Increased focus is another aspect of Kumon that isn't advertised much, and closely related to it is the feeling expressed by one father in California, regarding self-discipline, when he told me: "One of the most important things is for a youngster to learn discipline, to learn that he has to do this every day. I think it helps prepare a child for the real world. You know, the rest of life is full of standards and tests of one kind or another, but our schools have gotten away from that. It's not just their fault. Maybe as parents we've all gotten too easy-going. Kids who don't have personal standards probably haven't found them either at home or in school. The fact is, you need discipline and standards in life, and that's what we see in Kumon that really impresses us."

Parents of learning-impaired children as well as those with severely handicapped children point to the improvement in motor abilities as another big benefit. Other parents have pointed to their child's development of a greater sense of responsibility that comes with finishing Kumon homework every day. One woman told me how difficult it was to get her young son to start on his worksheets every day. After a couple of weeks she still wasn't sure whether she was making progress in instilling the sense that it was his responsibility to make sure his Kumon homework was done every day. Then one morning she woke up and went downstairs only to find that the Kumon worksheets were not on the table where she'd left them the night before. "I looked all over for them. Finally I found my son sitting in the kitchen making himself a bowl of cereal. 'What about your Kumon?' I asked him. 'Oh, I already did it,' he said.

And sure enough, he'd gotten up before me, done all his homework, and packed it up ready to go to school. I thought I was dreaming."

We've used Kumon as an instrument to help focus our children and teach them self-discipline. Terry realizes that his homework is required, that it's something we expect him to do. It's become a matter of self-discipline and self-control for him and he's grown right into it. I couldn't be happier.

—Roger Iger, father, Seattle

From people coast to coast, the comments I heard most often were that Kumon improves:

- self-confidence
- ability to concentrate
- self-discipline
- overall self-esteem

As one Midwestern mother said to me with a smile, "If that's all you get for your monthly fee, it's the best deal around."

Janie's progress has been very good; she's really taking responsibility for her own work. Her confidence has mounted and her study skills are improving steadily. I'm very impressed

—Georgia Hall, mother, Connecticut

What I'm seeing right now is a growth in self-esteem... his confi-

*dence level is way up. What do I think is responsible? I'm going
to have to say Kumon. I don't see any other variable in that time
period. Nothing has changed in his environment except Kumon.*

— Ralph Will, father, Virginia

Is there a 'downside' to Kumon?

This may seem an odd question at first, yet quite a few parents worry that the results of Kumon may be exactly what they've heard: ordinary kids discover that math can be interesting and fun, they start working harder and getting ahead of their normal school grade level, and suddenly you've got a Second Grade child working on high school math. We have all read about the twelve-year-old genius type who goes to Harvard because he can handle the academic material, but inside he's still just a twelve-year-old and cannot get along socially in this more adult environment. Although not too many of the parents I met seemed worried that their children were real geniuses, some were concerned that they might progress too fast for their own good, that they might become "math freaks" and miss out on their normal social development.

My only response, having talked to a lot of Kumon kids of various ages in many different parts of North America, is that they're the healthiest, happiest, most well-adjusted children I've met in a very long time. The only thing they're missing out on is anxiety over math classes and math tests. (And they are also missing out on the idea that education means just showing up for school, hanging

Kumon students have much in common besides math—self-confidence, self-esteem, and the ability and motivation to work on their own.

around with friends and never learning, and getting passed from one grade to the next until eventually they get a diploma.) If normal social development means spending time fooling around with friends never learning very much, then yes, they are missing out on that part of childhood, too. But that's all.

Since Kumon usually takes a maximum of thirty minutes out of a child's day—and for many children, twenty minutes or less—no one is going to "miss out" on anything except a half-hour of TV as a result of Kumon. And as for social adjustment, I met quite a few kids who were studying math in classes with older children and enjoying it. None of them complained about a lack of friends or any kind of social problem at school. Most of the kids remained in the same class at school, had the same friends they would have with or without Kumon, and got along just fine. The majority of them say they never even discuss Kumon with their school friends, and the ones who do discuss it say that no one makes them feel that they are "weird" just because they take a special math course. Almost all of the Kumon students that I spoke with said that their friends are impressed because they're so good in math. The reactions do not always stop there. Sometimes when their friends find out what the "secret" is, they ask their own parents if they can join Kumon.

So, if your child joins Kumon, will he or she turn into some kind of a "math freak?" The answer is no. Will Kumon cause your child to miss out on the normal activities for someone their age? No again. Many of the kids I met

The only difference between children in Kumon and other children is attitude and performance.

were like Matthew Christiansen in Maine, whose elementary school teacher was giving him 5th Grade math problems while he was in the 3rd Grade. Matthew thought that was just fine. He also swims a lot (he's in the Junior Olympics) and plays the piano. His sister, who studies Kumon math, skis, swims, ice skates, takes gymnastics, and plays the clarinet.

In fact, I hope my own son will someday become a "freak" like some of the kids I met. People like ten year-old John Liu from San Francisco. John is studying Japanese in Kumon as well as math. He's been in Kumon for about four years now, which does not seem to have hindered him in any way from singing, playing soccer, basketball, ping pong, and volleyball, and studying the violin. John is already working on simultaneous quadratic equations in Kumon Level J, which is pretty darn good for a ten year-old boy.

Then there's Amanda Gann from Portland, Maine. Amanda is only seven and she's been in Kumon for about three years, but she's just one level behind John Liu. Amanda is as happy and bubbly as any child her age in the United States She just happens to like doing algebra. I asked Amanda about Kumon: "I think it's a really great program. I hope to finish the whole program, all the way to the end." Is that all you do, study math all day long, I asked. "Oh, no," she replied, with that 'Adults say the silliest things' look, and patiently explained her other interests to me, "I play the piano, act in children's theater, and play a lot with my friends. I have lots of friends."

There are so many more children whose comments I

would like to include in this book. Hundreds, in fact. In every Kumon center you'll find kids just like them—happy and relaxed and enjoying school. Not because they're geniuses, but as one nine year-old told me, "Now I know I can do anything, no matter how hard, if I just try hard enough." Personally, if my own son learned just that one lesson, I would not even care what happened to his math scores.

When can I expect to see results?

This is a question that Kumon instructors often hear and just as often wish they didn't. First of all, the question implies that a parent wants some specific grade improvement in a fairly short time. While not impossible, this is unlikely. If a child studies conscientiously over a period of a year or so, Kumon will normally produce all kinds of results—including better grades in math—but these goals should not be short-term ones. Donna Ramesh, a Kumon instructor in Ohio, told me, "I have parents who come to me and say 'My son has to improve in math fast because he's got an algebra test in six weeks.' I have to tell them, 'That's not how it works. It takes time."

Indeed, the benefits of Kumon, such as improved school performance, concentration, self-discipline, and so on, are not a result of some magic lesson every child experiences three weeks after starting the program. All these benefits spring from steady, repeated study, and the development of new habits and new attitudes towards math. That takes time. Enrolling your child in Kumon in order to do better on a specific test a few months away is foolish. Enrolling your child in Kumon—and supporting that child's efforts yourself—in the hope of seeing better performance on tests from next year onwards, is a reasonable expectation.

Of course, no educational program can guarantee results, nor would Kumon ever make such a promise to either a parent or child. But there is an obvious, common-sense "guarantee" that underlies the Kumon Method. It is an old rule that applies to everything in life: if given a fair chance to succeed, people will improve in direct proportion to their efforts.

For some parents today, that kind of old-fashioned belief may seem quaint and outdated. Such parents may well prefer to look for short-term fixes to their children's educational problems. For most parents, the Kumon Method's "guarantee" makes sense. Why? Because it's the way we learned and the way we succeeded in school.

Many children today who are prepared to work hard are not given a fair chance to succeed. Even in areas where both the schools and the teachers are good, classes are often too big, there is too much pressure to move from one unit to another at a pace that inevitably leaves some kids behind, and little thought is given to motivating children from the earliest levels right through high school. Things are worse in places where the schools are badly equipped and badly understaffed. All too often the cards are stacked against the students no matter how much they may want to learn.

Kumon cannot change all that. It is not a school. It can only offer an alternate program to insure that students are learning the basics of math. Kumon says that if you start with carefully designed instructional materials, then remove all outside interference, including other students, class schedules, and even teachers, then every child will be guaranteed to progress as far and as fast as their own motivation will drive them. Add a comfortably low starting point to build confidence and show the child that every step up means 100% understanding of the previous steps, and the child's self-esteem begins to rise. As it does so, motivation also rises. In general, students who hated math before will find that they like the Kumon worksheet program, and students who liked math to begin with will usually charge into the program.

I asked Donna Ramesh if some parents put their children in Kumon and then take them out after a few months because they don't see immediate results. She told me that sadly this is often the case: "I feel sorry for parents who try Kumon for a few months and then stop, because they never got to see the benefits of it. It takes, at the very least, six months to see the first real benefits, and nobody's going to jump a full grade level in math in that time." At the same time, she noted that some of the other benefits—the change in attitude towards studying and the improvement in attention span, for example—do begin to appear within the first few months. If the student is being tested regularly in school, test scores may begin to improve after only six months. Every instructor I spoke with, however, emphasized that parents should not be thinking this way. If you are looking for quantifiable results to prove that your child's math ability is growing, wait at least a year. Many parents say that after the first year they were amazed at how much improvement they saw, and after the second year it was even more dramatic. As I traveled from center to center, many parents told me similar stories. Again and again people would say, "After we saw what it did for our older child in the first year, we put our other children into Kumon right away."

In other words, the Kumon Method is very results-oriented. Every minor step in Kumon requires proven speed and accuracy and every rise in level requires passing an achievement test. But the results that parents look for from Kumon take time. The message from instructors and parents alike is simple: "Be patient." Or as one mother told me, "Kumon isn't a quick fix. It's a lifelong fix—and that takes a little longer."

A Message From Toru Kumon

Parents frequently ask me, "What is the most important thing to remember in teaching my children?" I always reply with a question: How much confidence do you have in your children's potential? It is vitally important that we do not set artificial limits on what our children are capable of doing. I could give dozens of examples, but the first one that comes to mind is that of a mentally-handicapped girl who recently sat for a Japanese high school entrance exam (a very difficult test for any student). She was a good Kumon student and worked very hard at her studies, so we had no doubt that she would succeed. But the school officials were astounded. Clearly, because they knew of her learning disability they had developed false preconceptions about the limits of this girl's abilities.

My point is that children must be given every opportunity to succeed. It is a terrible shame for parents to give up on any child's abilities before he or she has had a real chance to grow. This is why I say that it is crucial for both parents and children to have a positive, "Let's try!" attitude. If you foster this attitude in your own children, you will be amazed at what they can do.

I firmly believe that this is our most important duty as parents. Then why do we, here at Kumon, promote mathematics?

Most people who have heard of the Kumon Method know that it helps children to do mathematical calculations faster than they could before. But the main objective of the Kumon Method is something more general: to give students the ability to study ahead of their grade level in school. When students study two or three years ahead of their grade level, they will not only master mathematics, but will also gradually learn how to study any subject on their own. In my experience, such children tend to develop certain common traits regardless of their backgrounds such as a tremendous natural curiosity, self-confidence, perseverance, and the ability to concentrate. These traits help children to develop not only their mathematical abilities, but their athletic and artistic abilities as well. Because of this, I believe that the skills and habits that the Kumon Method helps to build can improve a child's life in many ways.

At last count, more than 1.6 million children in Japan and 350,000 children in 27 countries around the world were studying with the Kumon Educational Method. I am especially pleased to see the Kumon Method spreading so quickly in North America because your society emphasizes making the most of individual abilities. In many schools there are systems for advanced students to skip grades, and there are special classes for gifted children. This tells me that the people of the United States and Canada also believe in the importance of developing children's abilities, regardless of their grade level.

On the other hand, there are still relatively few systems and institutions to help children whose scholastic abilities are below average. I sincerely hope that all children, whatever their level of scholastic ability, will have a chance to study with the Kumon Method because we consider it our mission to bring out the hidden potential in each and every child.

At present, there are 85,000 students studying Kumon in North America. Within ten years, I believe this number will surpass one million. As the real benefits of the program become apparent, it will continue to grow—to two million, three million and perhaps beyond. I look forward to the day when these millions of children—self-disciplined, self-motivated, and self-confident—will reward our faith in them by making their own contributions to society.

Toru Kumon

Osaka, Japan
October, 1993

Afterword

Over a year has passed since I first heard about Kumon. I started out knowing nothing more than the fact that my young son liked jigsaw puzzles with the Kumon name on them. I knew nothing at all about the Kumon Method, had never seen a Kumon center, nor had I talked with any parent or instructor involved with the program. In short, I was just about as "Kumon-ignorant" as I could be.

In the process of researching Kumon, I met with their executives in Osaka and Tokyo, interviewed the organization's leader, Toru Kumon, and visited both private Kumon centers and in-school programs from Maine to Los Angeles and Texas to Toronto.

I knew that as a journalist I should approach this task dispassionately, make up a list of questions to ask, interview people in an objective manner, and try to remain detached from the subject at least until I began to write. I will admit here and now that I failed completely. For I am also a parent, and my wife and I are starting to think long and hard about our own child's education. When I found myself traveling from one place to another meeting people involved with Kumon, I couldn't help but ask them the questions that most concerned me as a parent. If I reacted to some of their answers skeptically, it was not with the cynicism of a journalist on an assignment, but as a parent initially unable to believe all of the good things I heard from other parents about this thing called Kumon.

As is very obvious from this book, my skepticism—both personal and professional—melted away almost immediately. Despite all of the 7AM flights, the hotel meals and highway miles I would rather not remember, the most important part of my trip is something I can never forget—all of the great kids I met, their parents, and their Kumon instructors. They made a believer out of me.

I am delighted to have had the opportunity to research and write this book, and in the process, to learn about Kumon. I cannot say that Kumon is the answer to all the ills of our educational system...but, in my view, it certainly is a big step in the right direction.

D.R.

Kumon Offices

For those parents who would like to learn more about Kumon, I include a list of their offices to contact for further information, or visit our web site on the internet:

www.kumon.com

NORTH AMERICA

United States of America

Kumon U.S.A., Inc.
North American HQ

Glenpointe Centre East, Second Floor
300 Frank W. Burr Boulevard
Teaneck, New Jersey 07666

Tel: 201.928.0444
Fax: 201.928.0044

US East

New York/
New Jersey Offices

Glenpoint Centre East, Fifth Floor
300 Frank W. Burr Boulevard
Teaneack, NJ 07666

Tel: 201.928.0777
Fax: 201.928.1777

Boston Office

10 Elm Street
Danvers, MA 01923

Tel: 978.739.4227
Fax: 978.739.4727

Washington, D.C.
Office

Loehmann's Plaza, 5210 Randolph Road
Rockville, MD 20852

Tel: 301.231.6977
Fax: 301.231.6979

US Midwest

Chicago Office Two Continental Towers, Suite 109
1701 Golf Road
Rolling Meadows, IL 60008

Tel: 847.640.8384
Fax: 847.640.6340

Cincinnati Office Prospect Square
9708 Kenwood Road
Blue Ash, OH 45242

Tel: 513.745.0004
Fax: 513.745.9977

Detroit Office 28933 Woodward Avenue
Berkley, MI 48072

Tel: 248.541.7780
Fax: 248.541.7720

US South

Atlanta Office 6825 Jimmy Carter Blvd., Suite 1150
Norcross, GA 30071

Tel: 770.582.0013
Fax: 770.582.9388

Dallas Office 2140 East Southlake Boulevard, Suite I
Southlake, TX 76092

Tel: 817.329.6284
Fax: 817.421.1252

Houston Office 11777 Katy Freeway, Suite 190
Houston, TX 77079

Tel: 281.531.5026
Fax: 281.531.7516

US West

Los Angeles Office 300 Continental Boulevard, Suite 190
El Segundo, CA 90245

Tel: 310.333.1777
Fax: 310.414.0435

Honolulu Office 1357 Kapiolani Boulevard, Suite 1520
Honolulu, HI 96814

Tel: 808.949.6284
Fax: 808.949.7323

Phoenix Office 4710 East Elwood St., Suite 15
Phoenix, AZ 85040

Tel: 480.784.2992
Fax: 480.784.1677

San Francisco Office 111 Anza Boulevard, Suite 100
Burlingame, CA 94010

Tel: 650.347.8818
Fax: 650.347.8909

Seattle Office 10624 N.E. 37th Circle
Kirkland, WA 98033

Tel: 425.828.6284
Fax: 425.822.6769

Mexico

Mexico City Office Kumon Instituto de Educación
S.A. de C.V.
Blvd. Manuel Avila Camacho No. 37, Piso 5,
Col. Lomas de Chapultepe
C.P. 11000 Mexico D.F.

Tel: 5.281.2346
Fax: 5.281.3180

Canada

Kumon Canada Inc.
Toronto Office

344 Consumers Road
North York, Ontario M2J 1P8

Tel: 416.490.1722
Fax: 416.490.1694

Calgary Office

Lions Park Shopping Centre, 1503 19th Street N.W.
Calgary, Alberta T2N 2K2

Tel: 403.244.0157
Fax: 403.244.0857

Vancouver Office

Metrotower II
1203-4720 Kingsway
Burnaby, B.C. V5H 4N2

Tel: 604.454.1001
Fax: 604.454.1002

EUROPE

Germany

Düsseldorf Office

Kumon Deutschland GmbH
Alte Heerstrasse 7
41564 Kaarst

Tel: 02131.660034
Fax: 02131.63430

United Kingdom

Kumon Educational U.K. Co., Ltd.

London Office

Fifth Floor The Grange
100 High Street
Southgate London, UK N14 6ES

Tel: 181.447.9010
Fax: 181.447.9030

Manchester Office	Ground Floor Landmark House Station Road Cheadle Hulme Cheshire SK8 7GE Tel: 161.488.4988 Fax: 161.488.4980

Spain
Madrid Office

Kumon Instituto de Educación
de España S.A., Brava Murillo,
377 Primena Planta, Oficina C
28020 Madrid

Tel: 01.323.1053
Fax: 01.315.1579

SOUTH AMERICA

Brazil
São Paulo Office

Kumon Instituto de Educação S/C Ltda.
Rua Tomas, Carvalhal, 686, Paraiso,
Cep 04006-002 São Paulo-SP

Tel: 011.887.1869
Fax: 011.887.8251

Rio de Janeiro Office

Kumon Instituto de Educação S/C Ltda.
Avenida Presidente Antonio Carlos,
51, 3-Andar, Centro,
Cep 20010-010, Rio de Janeiro-RJ

Tel: 021.262.3203
Fax: 021.220.2547

Belo Horizonte Office

Kumon Instituto de Educação S/C Ltda.
Rua Maranhao, 339, 2° Andar,
Santa Efigenia
Cep 30150-330 Belo Horizonte-MG

Tel: 031.241.1733
Fax: 031.241.1275

Curitiba Office	Kumon Instituto de Educação S/C Ltda. Rua Emiliano Perneta, 297.5 Andar-Edif. Metropolitan Cep 80010-050 Curitiba-PR Tel: 041.322.4212 Fax: 041.225.6803
Porto Alegre Office	Kumon Instituto de Educação S/C Ltda. Avenida Plinio Brasil Milano, 203–Bairro Auxiliadora Cep 90520-002 Porto Alegre-RS Tel: 051.330.5777 Fax: 051.330.3815

Chile

Santiago Office	Kumon Instituto de Chile Ltda. AV. Holanda 160, Providencia, Santiago Tel: 2234.9288 Fax: 2234.9311

OCEANIA

Australia

Sydney Office	Kumon Institute of Education Kumon (Australia) Pty Ltd. Level 3, 22 Atchison Street St. Leonards, NSW 2065 Tel: 02.9438.2640 Fax: 02-9438.1848
Melbourne Office	Kumon Institute of Education Kumon (Australia) Pty Ltd. Level 3, 40 Albert Rd., South Melbourne, VIC 3205 Tel: 03.9696.1566 Fax: 03.9696.2619

Brisbane Office	Kumon Institute of Education Kumon (Australia) Pty Ltd. 47 Warner Street, Fortitude Valley QLD 4006 Tel: 07.3257.3590 Fax: 07.3257.3596
Perth Office	Kumon Institute of Education Kumon (Australia) Pty Ltd. Level 9, 251 Adelaide Terrace Perth, WA 6000 Tel: 09.325.8900 Fax: 09.325.8909

ASIA

Japan
KUMON Headquarters   Kumon Institute of Education
5-6-6 Nishinakajima,
Yodogawa-ku, Osaka 532

Tel: 06.838.2619
Fax: 06.838.2705

Hong Kong
Hong Kong Office

Kumon Hong Kong Co. Ltd.
15 Floor, Luk Kwok Centre,
72 Gloucester Road, Wan Chai

Tel: 852.890.6533
Fax: 852.894.8285

Malaysia
Singapore Office

Kumon Singapore Pte. Ltd.
5 Shenton Way #23-09/10
UIC Building, 068808

Tel: 65.225.8813
Fax: 65.225.1722

Malaysia Office	Kumon Asia Pte. Ltd. Malaysia Branch No. 2D-5, Jalan SS6/6 Kelana Jaya 47301 Petaling Jaya Selangor Darul Ehsan, Kuala Lumpur Tel: 03.7061869 Fax: 03.7061876

Philippines
Manila Office

Kumon Philippines, Inc.
Unit 12-A, Multinational Bancoproration
Center, 6505 Ayala Avenue
Makati City, Metro Manila

Tel: 02.845.0193
Fax: 02.845.0963

China
Shanghai Office

Shanghai Kumon Educational
Software Co., Ltd.
Branch of Pudong New Area Education College
485 Miao Jing Road
Chuansha County
Changhai City

Tel: 86.21.5898.2207
Fax: 86.21.5898.2476

Guangdong Office

Guangdong Kumon Science & Technogoloy
Intelligence Co. Ltd.
Room 706, 708 Building of the Micro-Organism
Research Institute Chinese Academy of Science
(Guangdong Branch) 100, Xianlie Zhong Rd.
Guangzhou

Tel: 86.20.8760.4566
Fas: 86.20.8766.8082

JOINT VENTURES

Taiwan

Taipei Office

Kumon Cultural Enterprise Co., Ltd.
Chi Kuang Center for Banking &
Commerce, 5th Floor
48 Min Chuan West Road
104, Taipei

Tel: 02.543.2391
Fax: 02.541.4549

Taichung Office

Kumon Cultural Enterprise Co., Ltd.
Rockefeller B Bldg. 9F., 2
No. 629, Sec. 1, Chung De Rd.
N. Ward, Taichung

Tel: 04.238.5677
Fax: 04.237.2407

Kaohsiung Office

Kumon Cultural Enterprise Co., Ltd.
20F-1, No. 56 Min Sheng Rd.
Kaohsiung

Tel: 07.227.2961
Fax: 07.227.3291

Indonesia

Jakarta Office

P.T. Kumon Indonesia Lestari
Wisman Anugraha Ground Floor
JL. Taman Kemang 32B
Jakarta Selatan, 12730

Tel: 021.797.5021
Fax: 021.797.5076

Seoul Office
(Affiliated Operations)

Kumon Institute of Education Co., Ltd.
904 Cygnus B/D, 7 Mookyo-Dong
Chung-Gu, Seoul

Tel: 02.754.6143
Fax: 02.754.6144

South Africa
Johannesburg Office   Kumon Education South Africa (Pty) Ltd.
                               1 Ninth St. Houghton 2198
                               P.O. Box 1417 Houghton 2041
                               Johannesburg

For information on Kumon centers in the following countries, please contact the corresponding office:

Austria	Düsseldorf Office
France	Düsseldorf Office
Italy	Düsseldorf Office
Hungary	Düsseldorf Office
Switzerland	Düsseldorf Office
Columbia	São Paolo Office
Peru	São Paolo Office
All Other Countries	Osaka Headquarters

About the Author

David Russell is an investigative journalist who has lived and worked in Japan since 1982. In addition to stints as a writer and editor for both of Japan's top financial news organizations, he has also contributed articles on everything from American society to the future of the Japanese economy. His articles have appeared in publications ranging from the *International Herald Tribune* to the *Harvard Business Review* and in several well-known Japanese periodicals. In addition to being a working author, who has written or co-authored several books on subjects related to international business, David Russell is the Managing Editor of *Tokyo Business Today*, an English-lanugage monthly.